The Football and Real Al...
What's it all ...

The website

www.footballandrealaleguide.co.uk.

The website is a place for you, the reader, to get involved in the process of nominating pubs and telling me interesting things about the people that make them so successful. If you want to be in the guide then the website is there for you to get involved.

I am sure that there are many other great pubs that didn't make the guides this year and with your help we will make next years guides both better and more interesting to read.

Hosted by 1and1.com it has details of the work in progress, a beer forum and contact details so that you can get involved in talking real ale and footie whenever you wish. It also includes my Pub of the Week and fun competitions.

The winner of the competition, who wins two away tickets for this season, was GEOFF CLARKE of Wednesbury.

The editor / publisher

WHEN lifelong Bristol Rovers fan Richard Stedman was pondering a change of career, he was asked what were the two great loves of his life. It didn't take him long to come up with the answers -football and beer.

"When I went to see people from the Enterprise Agency, I told them I thought I'd like to run a pub - and they just laughed and told me to forget it. They said to go away and think of the two things I loved most in life and then to try and come up with something involving them both, which is where the idea for the books came from.

"I select what I believe are the best three pubs to visit if, like me, you enjoy tip-top real ale as well as watching your team away from home.

"There will rarely be agreement as to what is the best, so I am spending the next few months visiting all pubs near the grounds and talking to the locals about their experiences of football fans who like to visit a pub, quaff the ales on offer and banter about the game."

He is also looking for feedback from supporters nominating their favourite real ale pubs and can be contacted via his website www.footballandrealaleguide.co.uk.

Chris Swift Bristol Evening Post (Dec. 2004)

What makes a good real ale and football pub?

This guide is compiled with the real ale fan in mind. It is a real ale guide for away footie fans, looking for great ale rather than the company of fellow away fans.

I have tried to get a selection of pubs and locations so that all beer hunter can find something to suit their taste.

For some it is the opportunity to sample local brews. not available in their home town Others look for a location very close to the ground. For some the most important factor is the range of beers, seeking microbrews in particular.

Others seek out the football friendly factors, appreciating a good chat with similar fans in their own pub, often building friendships that last for years.

Whether it is a pub crawl, or a good meal with their pint, in every case it is the people who make a great pub. The Gu- v'nor is often the key to finding a great welcome and great beer.

Happy hunting

Stedders 2005

PREMIERSHIP LEAGUE TOWNS

	Points	Top scorers
Newcastle	8 - 9	Free Press, Cumberland Arms, Tyne Bar.
Sunderland	10 -11	Saltgrass Inn, Kings Arms, Fitzgerald's
London	12 - 21	Lamb, Wenlock Arms, Compton Arms, Market Porter, Sir Richard Steeles, Princess Louise, Dove, Victoria, Carpenters Arms, Head Of Steam, Oakdale Arms, Old Bank of England.
Manchester	22 - 25	The Crescent, Peveril of the Peak, Jolly Angler, Smithfield Hotel, Beer House, Hare and Hounds.
Liverpool	26 - 29	Baltic Fleet, Fly in the Loaf, The Philharmonic, Dr. Duncan's, Ship and Mitre, White Star.
Bolton	30 - 31	Bob's Smithy, Hen and Chickens, Howcroft Inn.
Portsmouth	34 - 35	Sir Loin of Beef, Artillery Arms, Florence Arms.
Birmingham	36 -39	City Tavern, Old Fox, Bartons Arms, Old Moseley Arms, Anchor, White Swan.
West Bromwich	42 -43	Vine, Wheatsheaf, Old Crown
Wigan	44 - 45	Bowling Green, Anvil, Swan and Railway
Blackburn	46 - 47	Navigation, The Adelphi, Fielden Arms.
Middlesbrough	48 - 49	Dr Brown's, Crown Hotel, Ship
A weekend in the Championship	51 - 54	Sheffield
A weekend in Division One	55 - 57	Bristol
Division Two best town	58 - 59	Shrewsbury

Three B's Brewery

SEASONAL VARIETY

CUPID'S FUEL
(Valentine's
Day)   4.5%

EASTER GOLD
(Easter)   4.0%

BEE HAPPY
(Summer)   4.3%

BOMMY BEER
(Bonfire Week)   4.5%

SANTA'S SKINFUL
(Christmas)   4.0%

Heaven in a glass

ADDITIONAL ALES

PINCH NOGGIN
(Bitter)   4.6%

KNOCKER UP
(Porter)   4.8%

SHUTTLE ALE
(Strong Pale Ale)   5.2%

NEDDY WAPP
This new beer has been com-
missioned solely for the Pack
Horse Belthorn Nr Blackburn.
                        4.3%

STOKER'S SLAKE ABV 3.6%
A traditional dark mild, roast malt aromas and creamy chocolate notes.

When in the North West the Brewery ales to search for is;-

Three B's Brewery

Unit 5, Laneside Works
Stockclough Lane
Feniscowles
Blackburn
BB2 5JR

Contact
Tel / Fax . 01254 207686
Mobile 07752282570
www.threebsbrewery.co.uk

How to use the pages

Maps

Beware The maps are not to scale

The maps identify streets local to the pubs and best routes to the ground. They also show routes from the main railway station to pubs rather than the grounds. The description on the "shorts" is my summary of, and recommendation for, the real ale scene in the town.

Norwich

This city has it all, including busy pubs very close to the ground. You cannot fail here, so my recommendation is to find the Fat Cat early and then go nearer the ground. You won't want to waste time on the way, get here and feast on genuine choice. For the tourist style day the Ribs is a great location.

Guide entries

The information is correct on the date of visit but may have changed. I give the beers on tap on the day of my visit. They are written in order of their appearance on the bar. You will have to judge the beer range from that. One would expect that if a winter beer is on when I visit, then seasonals will be there when you are there. I do not include the beers that landlords say they have just finished or "will be on tomorrow"

The main bit

I have described the pub as I saw it on the day of my visit. This may have changed. I hope to give a flavour of the pub. In italics are comments made to me via the website / interviews / comment cards etc. The names used are those that they chose to use. If there is no name it is from a person who didn't want to be quoted. I cannot guarantee their accuracy but I include them if they add to my entry in an interesting way.

Owner of the pub. - If it is part of a chain I try to give it but most are freehouses. Some abbreviations are used, e.g. W+D for Wolverhampton and Dudley.

G - Guvnor' To save any argument I give the name of either the landlord, / manager / owner of the pub. i.e. whoever the guvnor wanted to be held responsible at the time.

F - Food The pubs describe their own food. if not then I give the time of opening on a Saturday. For evening games then you have to take it to chance as this often varies. No **F** = no food

W - Website I give the website for the pub. I do not guarantee they are working or up to date

S - Smoking policy is described as at the time of my visit.

Photographs

With one exception all photographs were taken by myself and on the day of my visit.

Symbols with the photos.

In each guide I have tried to identify the very best pubs by allocating 11 Championship pub awards. They are indicated by the symbol shown here. There is one such award for the best in each category as indicated in the description. A pub having this award would be good in any town having;-

- a range of excellent ales,
- an interesting selection of ales,
- A friendly, welcoming atmosphere
- recommendations in real ale guides and web sites and
- a beer policy that encourages the promotion of real ale

PLUS A specialism in one or more of the award categories.

Award Categories

Within 10 minutes to the ground
The pub is within easy walking distance of the ground, perhaps having spaces in a car park or convenient safe parking near the pub.

Pub for food.
Many pubs are specialising in food but this award is for a pub that has something different, perhaps a theme for the food or gearing the menu on the day for footie fans. The food should be reasonably priced and obviously recommended by fans as of good quality

Brewery Tap
The pub is an independent brewery tap and showcases its beer with a full range of ales.

Street corner local
This pub has a street corner location or be located in a residential area thus serving local regulars who use the pub during non match days.

High Street / Station boozer
The pub that wins this award must either be within two minutes walk of the main station or the High Street of the town. It will be welcoming to people who are often unfamiliar to the regulars.

Historic pub
The historic nature can be defined either by the rare pub architecture, historical context or perhaps of beer history value.

Microbrew champion
This pub will normally only serve regional or national microbrews, offering beers that will be something of a surprise to the not so casual beer visitor.

Footie fans pub
The regulars in the pub win this award. They create a welcome to away fans through their general welcome and the way they accept the away fans as lovers of real ale and their team.

Pub with a view
The view might be through the window of the pub or its setting might be in an attractive tourist location.

Community pub
The pub is a place where the Guv'nor encourages local community spirit perhaps by running quiz, darts or footie teams, maybe they are charity fund raising champions or involved in keeping the village in which they are located alive.

Loads of real ale pub
Not only will the pub have 6 plus real ales always available but the numbers using the pub means the turnaround of ales is constant. You can go in for a couple of hours and try many beers of the type you like while your friends are sampling their different style of craft ale.

The Pub of the year was selected by deciding which pub would fit into the most categories.

Symbols under the photos

sp   sk   jb   pg   d

There are five abbreviations that might appear here. No abbreviation means the pub doesn't have any T.V., music, pub games or good disabled access etc.

cp - car park
sp - street parking
mp - only metre or paid car parking nearby.

tv or sky.

Jb - juke box
bm - background music selected by the pub

pg -pub games like darts pool etc played here

d - disabled access is rated by the landlord as good or excellent.

BWV - Beer when visited plus date of visit

LEAGUE TABLES

The guide is arranged in order of what I think are the best real ale town to the worst. The best towns has many more real ale pubs than those listed in this guide and the choice of ales ranges from nationals to local microbrews. The most important factor however is that the pubs selected offer a range of drinking locations and are friendly locations for away fans to enjoy without any hassle. The other guides in the Football and real ale guide series are similarly arranged and included are the tables. The league tables are compiled for the 2004 -05 season.

Extra towns

As the Premiership has fewer teams I also include pages for the best weekend away towns in the country. Perhaps a cup game will entice you to spend some time in the town or you might use it as an alternative location away from the town in which your team is playing.

SOURCES USED TO COMPILE THE GUIDES

A good day out finding real ale before and after the game might involve using these sources. Before I visited each town these are the sources I used to narrow down my search.

Books / guides.

Campaign for Real Ale, Good Beer Guide 2004

Campaign for Real Ale, Good Beer Guide 2005

A.A. The Pub Guide 2004

CAMRA Local pub guides throughout the country.

Rough Guides The Rough Guide to Britain (2002)

Websites

www.thebeerguide.co.uk

www.pub-explore.com

www.beerfestivals.org

www.footballgroundguide.dial.pipex.com

www.camra.org.uk

www.beermad.org.uk

www.beerintheevening.com

www.dafts.co.uk (Darlington F.C.)

www.park-road.u-net.com (London Clarets)

www.theawayend.com

and of course comments on

www.footballandrealaleguide.co.uk

The best of these guides is that produced by Steve Duffy, Ted Blair and their mates at Darlington. It has masses of information on good real ale pubs in the lower divisions. Come on Darlo get into the top divisions so we can all share in some wider detail. Their guide to their home town is included below as an example of their website descriptions.

Real ale
For real ale fans, <u>**Number Twenty 2,**</u> *22 Coniscliffe Road* takes some beating. The runner up in the *Darlington CAMRA town pub of the year 2004*, "22's" has an excellent selection of beers and wines, with a pub grub and a separate canteen area during the day. Regular featured beers include Village brewery ales, but others change regularly. Popular with an over 30s crowd at night and nicknamed *Jurassic Park* by those who get squiffy on two Bacardi Breezers. Just one type of lager and no spirits or silly alco-pops. No music, a "fine for charity" for use of mobile phones. Despite or perhaps because of the restrictions, this is a relaxed place for beer and conversation. *Open from 12pm, closed Sundays and Mondays.* <u>Click for map</u>

Voted yet again in 2004 *Darlington CAMRA Pub of the Year* and it's hard to argue. Well worth trying to find this quirky and hospitable bar down an alleyway, <u>**The Quaker Cafe,**</u> *2 Mechanics Yard, off High Row, entrance next to Binns* has a small real ale bar downstairs, which now has more regularly changing guest ales - now a choice of 10 hand-pulls, not forgetting the Quaker Ghost Ale regular - the spirits don't just come in bottles at this bar. Also now does bar lunches on Saturday's. *Very football-friendly and open from 11am matchdays.* It recently won a reprieve after being threatened with "refurbishment" into something far less appealing.
"The Quaker Caff" is in the *Good Beer Guide* and in recent months has had a slight refurbishment, with a few more lights and tables for lunches downstairs too. Licensees Steve and Lynda know their beer and there's always a warm welcome for football fans before the game. <u>Click for map</u>

Premiership award winners

	Pub	Town
Within 10 minutes to the ground	Sir Loin of Beef	Portsmouth
Pub for food	The Vine	West Bromwich
Brewery Tap	Coach and Horses	Norwich
Street corner local	Howcroft	Bolton
Town High Street / Station boozer	Ship and Mitre	Liverpool
Historic pub	Hare and Hounds	Manchester
Microbrew champion	The Crescent	Manchester
Footie fans pub	Artillery Arms	Portsmouth
Pub with a view	Free Trade	Newcastle
Community pub	Cumberland Arms	Newcastle
Loads of real ale pub	Fat Cat	Norwich

Pub of the year 2004 - 05

The award goes to the pub which meets most of the criteria above.

THE COACH AND HORSES

NORWICH

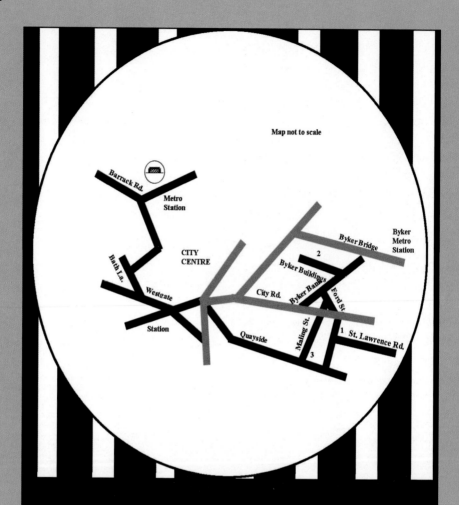

Map not to scale

Barrack Rd.

Metro
Station

Byker Bridge

Byker
Metro
Station

CITY
CENTRE

2

Byker Buildings

Bath La.

Westgate

City Rd.

Byker Banks

Ford St.

Station

Quayside

Malling St.

1 St. Lawrence Rd.

3

Newcastle

The Cathedral of St James' dominates the skyline. On matchdays the Toon army is everywhere and a great time can be had in its city pubs. I however would head along the riverfront to the renewed Ouseburn Valley area and have my own personal pub crawl.

1 Free Trade Freehouse   2 Cumberland Arms F   3 Tyne Bar Freehouse

sp   jb   sp   bm   pg   sp   jb

1 Free Trade Freehouse

St Lawrence Rd, NE6 1AP
G Ted Pye
F Specialist sandwiches from 11
T 0191 2655764
S Smoking throughout

BWV 12.1.05 Rudgate **Viking,** Hadrian and Border **Farne Island,** Wylam **Bohemian,** Jarrow **McConnell's Stout,** Mordue **Workie Ticket**

When all around was being gentrified the Free Trade opened up its windows, painted the walls, sold real ale and put on live music. It became a place to come early to enjoy the views, or later to immerse yourself in neo-Geordie pub culture. i.e. locals necking Newcastle Brown? *Your minds eye says walk on, go in and you won't trust your prejudiced views again. The campaign activists will need to protect this pub. Go and watch the sun set after a game.* The Free Trade is a great pub heaped in the traditions of good music, good real ale and fantastic locals who know how to enjoy a good time. I just had to take a couple of visits to fully appreciate the strengths of the place. It was very relaxed having a wide range of customers. My plan is to revisit in the summer where a great afternoon could be spent admiring all that is of beauty in the Tyne Valley, perhaps looking out across the river as well!

2 Cumberland Arms F

Byker Buildings, NE6 1LD
G Jo Hodson
F Good bar food from 12.30
T 0191 2656151
S Smoking throughout
W www.thecumberlandarms.co.uk

BWV 12.1.05 Jarrow **JB Bitter,** Wylam **Rapper,** Knights **Cider**

A pub where you never know quite what to expect. They offer the choice of having your beer served the traditional way straight from the wood or through hand pumps. The website says that they have a great reputation for good traditional music in the upstairs room. This is my favourite Newcastle pub and that is saying something because there are masses of great pubs in the town. What you are guaranteed is great company, gentle humour and quality real ale. It has some interesting ways to guarantee good comfort and create a reflective atmosphere. A lending library, a bring your own instrument policy, plus advertising the beers on a good website all make you feel that the locals cherish their pub. A great evening was had chatting with local characters, I felt that the conversation was as passionate about local issues as was my love of the choice of ales and now real ciders. A top pub at the top of a worthwhile climb from the river and a guide award winner.

3 Tyne Bar Freehouse

Maling St, Byker, NE6 1LP
G Martin Eve
F Sandwiches and hot Panini's from 12
T 0191 2652550
S Smoking throughout
W www.thetyne.com

BWV 12.1.05 Mordue **Workie Ticket,** Jarrow **Rivet Catcher,** Font Valley **Hoppy New Beer,** Wylam **Magic**

This is a different, almost American feeling bar, i.e. dimly lit and with free jukebox, and music posters. The atmosphere was just atmospheric. My visit coincided with the cellar being flooded by water backing up the Ouseburn so I have to rely on others who say the pub is actually light and airy. Ale was still on as the tide fell, no lager though. Now that's an idea for CAMRA to encourage, flood your cellars, turn off any electric pumps and watch the lager drinkers sample real ale for the first time. (Perhaps not) It can get crowded but is a place to relax after the stroll along the waterfront. Its website revels in quotes of how good it is. The Tyne Bar also has a great reputation for live music, having the space for bands in the larger bar. The best bet would be to enjoy the beer in the beer garden under the bridge and plan an assault of the hill to the other two pubs in this guide.

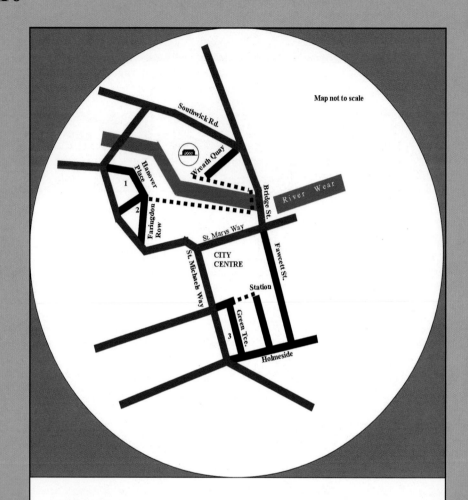

Sunderland

Sunderland has a growing, almost "underground" real ale movement going on. While the city centre has choice that extends north towards Roker and the Stadium of Light. My choice concentrates on the Deptford area where the revolution is in full swing.

1 Saltgrass Inn Punch

2 Kings Arms Freehouse

3 Fitzgerald's

sp

cp   sk   bm   pg

mp   sk   bm

37 Hanover Place, Deptford SR4 6BY
G Daryl Frankland
F Bar food / snacks - restaurant menu from 12
T 0191 565 7229
S Smoking in bar, non smoking lounge / restaurant

BWV 13.1.05 **Sleighbells** Caledonian **Deuchars IPA**, **Bass**, Black Sheep **Bitter**, Westons **Scrumpy**.

Do you remember seaside, scrimshaw and seashell pubs? Well in Deptford, among the riverside warehouses you can find the Saltgrass. It is dark and comfortable, intimate and cosy, a place to revel in winter warmth. The banter alone is well worth the taxi ride. Andrew of Houghton praises the *great pre match atmosphere* Similarly John Watson of York says *what more could you want, than well kept beers with friendly staff and regulars and a good real fire?* While *the fire keeps some in on freezing days when the lads are playing below par* for Dave it is *the barmaids who are dead fit* Daryl is one of those landlords who sell their businesses as their passion. Any real ale fan will learn masses spending time in his company. The guest ale choice is always reliably good, mixing well known brands with rarer regional ales.

1 Hanover Place, SR4 6BU
G Lucie Young
F From 12 Sandwiches before, free hot soup and roll after.
T 0191 5679804
S Possible no smoking area on demand

BWV 13.1.05 Glentworth **White**, Ossett **Silver King**, Concertina **One Eyed Jack**, Anglo Dutch **On T''Way**, Wentworth **Bumble Bee**.

This is a place to find rare micro brews, *that are tip top and blows your doors in. (Steve Potts)* The Guv'nor is a relentless hunter of real ale and the customers come from afar to sample. 6-10 at the weekend. My visit was one of my highlights of the years research, thanks to the easy conversation and genuine warmth of the bar flies. As Jean Downey says *It's great because of the pre match banter between friends and strangers alike. After the game for warm down and hot soup plus fab bar staff.* Mickie Downey goes on to say that *it has a great pre match atmosphere, full of football families of all ages and friendly away fans.* They will, however, spin some tales of fans getting a boat to the game, better to walk via the river side path or get a taxi. It has *good beer, good crack, live football and I go (Kipper).* It can't have everything I suppose.

10-12 Green Terrace, SR1 3PZ
G Matt Aldis
F From 11
T 0191 5670852
S Separate smoking areas
W fitzgeralds.co.uk

BWV 13.1.05 Archers **Pixie Juice**, Ushers **Winter Storm**, Cains **Raisin**, Morland **Original**, Orkney **Skull Splitter**, Archers **Scatty Cow**, Thwaites **Original**, Harvieston **Jack the Lad**, Brains **SA**, Westons **Country Perry**.

Ten constantly changing beers are found here in an area popular with both young and old. This pub changes as the different groups come and go. It is sometimes very crowded, yet at other times it offers real tranquility. There is always a quality selection of real ales particularly for northern ales. It is simply the best for real ale in the city centre. It is quite a large pub, offering separate sections rather than rooms. Apparently the wireless internet access is proving popular with business trade and regulars alike. I enjoyed sitting in the rear of the pub chatting with a couple of old timers who were keen to stress the friendliness of the staff as a major factor in it being their choice. They were also keen to make sure they had a seat before the younger crowd came in for their usual evening beer and chat up session.

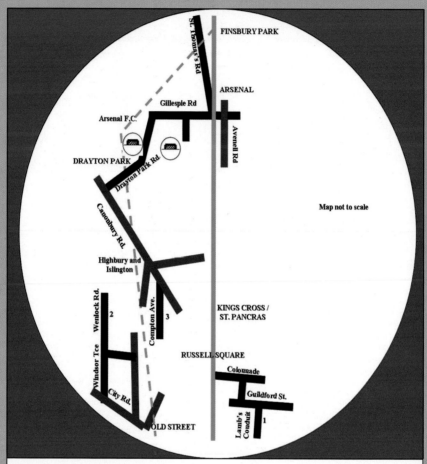

Changes from other lines to Piccadilly Line

Kings Cross - Victoria, Northern, Hammersmith and City, Metropolitan, Circle and mainline

Holborn - Central

Leicester Square - District

Piccadilly Circus - Bakerloo

Green Park - Jubilee and Victoria

South Kensington - Circle, District

1 Lamb Youngs

mp

4 Lambs Conduit St, WC1N 3LZ
G Michael and Joanne Hehir
F From 12
T 020 74050713
S No smoking in the snug

BWV 12.04 Youngs **Winter Warmer, Bitter, Special, Christmas Ale.**

This is a comfortable and traditional London ale house that has an air of reflective calm and a murmur of secretive discussion. The mix of students and nurses alongside the well heeled professionals gives this a feeling of being a place to see and be seen. I visited the Lamb's Conduit in early afternoon and the pub was habited by a very friendly range of people, some like me just enjoying its cosiness, others meeting friends as a regular event, chatting around the bar. It's back street location means it is a bit of a rare find for the masses and helps to create a feeling of "Village" exclusivity while in parallel roads there is masses of hustle and bustle. The classic London pub architecture prevails in screens and dark wooden furniture. Quite often you will find players from local five a side teams quenching their collective thirsts after a game on the nearby Astroturf. It offers a great alternative as the connections via the Piccadilly line are endless.

2 Wenlock Arms Freehouse

mp   sk   bm   pg

26 Wenlock Rd N1 7TA
G Steven Barnes and John Williams
F Good pub sarnies and pies from 12
T 020 7608 3406
S Smoking throughout
W Wenlock_arms.co.uk

BWV 6.12.04 Adnams **Best** Pitfield **East Kent** Goldings **Grainstone** Rutland **Panther Mild** Harveys **Armada** Nelsons **Friggin' Yuletide** Titanic **Premium** Pictish **Porter**

Follow the taxis of the city workers from Old St station and you find this glory in regenerating Hoxton. Small and comfortable, the pub has a lively, yet almost reverential feel. Easily the most recommended London pub to my website its reputation goes far beyond the local area. You are more likely to find an old mate from a real ale festival than your average crafty cockney. Steven and Will run a top boozer .Whether sitting at the bar or squeezing onto a table you are guaranteed a good real ale find. The turnover of ales is so great that a longer session will bring up surprises from rarer microbreweries as well as national seasonal ales. The Wenlock is simply a top notch boozer yet is still a locals community pub as witnessed by the pub cricket and darts teams.

3 Compton Arms, Greene King

mp   sk

4 Compton Ave, N1 2XD
G Eileen Shelock
F Freshly home made food, sausage and mash a speciality.
T 020 73596883
S Smoking throughout

BWV 6.12.04 Greene King **IPA, Abbot, Morland Original Rev. James.**

The Compton Arms is my idea of pre footie match heaven. Small enough for you to be recognised as a non regular, yet friendly enough to guarantee that you can enjoy the pub without any hassle. For the locals this pub is geared up for the sports fan with a TV in every corner. However, it is a proper community local, very popular and keeping its "village" identity. Come on a non Arsenal home day and the locals will make you welcome with tales of glories present. If fact it is best to check out if Arsenal are away because it is likely to be too busy if they are at home. My choice would be to find this pub on an early evening after a game or as part of a weekend real ale ticking jaunt. Perhaps a beer and some food in the courtyard or a read of the Sunday papers before heading back home the next day. Whenever you get here, make sure that you do, it would be a crime to miss sampling such a friendly back street ale house.

London

4 Market Porter Freehouse | 5 Sir Richard Steeles F | 6 Princess Louise Samuel Smiths

mp   bm   pg   d   mp   tv   bm   pg   mp

4 Market Porter

9 Stoney St, SE1 9AA
G Nick Turner
F Restaurant upstairs serving traditional food from 12
T 020 7407 2495
S Smoking throughout

BWV 6.12.04 Harveys **Best,** Mauldons **Pickwick, Suffolk Pride,** Archers **Black Jack Porter,** Hardy and Hansons **Dark Mild,** , Daleside **Shrimpers,** Bath Ales **Gem, Barnstormer**

Is this London's most "ticked" pub? Always busy, rightly popular, this wood panelled boozer with ever changing beer range draws city gents and beer tourists to the home of the Porters. This is either the ideal starting point for a London crawl, or a last stopping off point before suffering the south east train crawl. I love the buzz of the place, I found a space in the corner and, as a country boy at heart, just immersed myself in the sheer glory of big city conversation, much of it football related. The added extra of the Market Porter is its location in the heart of Borough Market. For a change why not get there for breakfast if you are travelling a distance or tie in your beer hunt with a stroll among the stalls. The most recommended London guide entry it is always busy and offers quality in all it does.

5 Sir Richard Steeles

97 Haverstock Hill, NW3 4RL
G Kirk McGrath
F Thai food from 12
T 020 74831261
S Smoking throughout

BWV 6.12.04 Flowers **Original IPA** Greene King **Old Speckled Hen.**

This was well worth Ben's local recommendation. Arsenal and Chelsea fans were found here, chatting in the library style rooms with impressive frescos and picture windows to help dream of present glories This is *a clubby pub*, as it should be, open to all ages and attitudes, *truly excellent.* Between Belsize park and Chalk Farm tube stations the walk is best taken down hill from the former to the latter I could imagine this being a great locals pub as it was apparent the place was populated by people who knew each other well yet were quick to make the new boy visitor welcome. As a local community pub it runs several footie teams that sometimes include some well known former stars, that should make for a great Sunday lunchtime session for the older fans. Bring a friend and enjoy the beauty of the building or just yourself and enjoy its calming atmosphere. It will, however be packed in the evening and at weekends. Cheers Ben.

6 Princess Louise

208 High Holborn WC1V 7BW
G Campbell Mackay
F Sandwiches and ploughman's from 12
T 020 74058816
S Smoking throughout

BWV 25.1.05 ,Samuel Smiths **OBB**

Only 1 real ale? But what an ale, and what a place to drink it. There are many pumps, all serving OBB, the eye is also drawn to quality in the bottle cabinets The pub features the full range of Sam Smiths bottled ales and also satisfies the continental beer fan. Most impressive is the price of the ale; no London extortion rates here and no sign of cheap booze cruisers either The bar itself is large and surrounded on all sides by ample comfortable seating. Close to Holborn station it is well worth getting in for a quiet pint before heading North or alternatively making it the place to get over the post match tube experience before heading off to the train home. References to this pub always mention the Victorian toilets, I would rather comment on the ornate mirrors and wall carvings. *I have yet to go in there and not be impressed by the friendliness of the staff and the price of the ale.* A place to meet up with mates as all main line stations being easily accessible.

7 Birkbeck Tavern Freehouse

sp   sk   jb   pg   d

Langthorne Rd. E11 4HL
G Roy Leach
F Various rolls from 12
T 02085392584
S Smoking throughout

BWV 25.1.05 Rita's **Special (House Brew)**, Barnsley **Oakwell Bitter**, Skinners **Betty Stogs**, St. Austell **Tinners**

The Birkbeck Tavern is the grand daddy of London lower division pubs. Any supporters of larger teams on a weekend away need to make a tour to find this pub as you are unlikely to play Leyton Orient and have an excuse to visit. Landlord Roy goes the extra mile to make you feel welcome as do the football mad locals. Operating a genuine two day maximum to turn round to a new ale it is popular with the "Pigs Ear" real ale crew and away fans who often phone in advance to check out the brews on offer. They are often surprised but rarely disappointed, over 300 different beers a year have been on offer. *One of my favourite haunts before a game.* It is something very special. The atmosphere on matchdays is just perfect, totally friendly, especially on balmy summers days when the garden comes into its own. In the middle of winter the genuine Leyton warmth comes to warm the cockles of your footie heart.

8 Churchill Arms Fullers

mp   sk   bm

119 Kensington Church St. W8 7LN
G Jerry O'Brien
F Thai restaurant from 12
T 020 77274242
S Smoking in the pub only

BWV 6.12.04 Fullers **London Pride, Chiswick, ESB, Jack Frost**

In the heart of café and bistro land the Churchill represents tradition without pretence. The Irish roots come through in the sports themes, particularly Gaelic football and London Irish rugby. The love of real ale is easy to notice within the conversations of its diverse clientele. *The best pint of ESB I have ever tasted* (Overheard in pub - Mike) This is a blooming good pub winning London in Bloom awards. *It is a lovely pub, great beer, really friendly bar staff, (I'm always a sucker for gorgeous, Irish girls!) Its also a great place for a last few pints, as you can leave at around 11 o'clock & still get to Paddington for the last train home. (Nigel C Bristol)* Of note for historians are references to Winny and wartime memorabilia. For TV sports fans the television is more likely to be coveted by Rugby fans rather than those who want their fill of Premiership footie. And then there is the Thai food to sample after a game.

9 Mad Bishop and Bear

mp   tv   bm   d

The Lawn, Paddington Station W2 1HB
G Clare Gage
F From 7.30 in the morning
T 020 74022441
S Separate smoking areas

BWV 20.12.04 Fullers **London Pride, ESB, London Porter, Chiswick.**

In my opinion this is the best designed London station bar. It takes elements of classic pub design (tiled floors and mirrors etc.) and integrates them into a large, modern, terminus waiting bar complete with two plasma screens for TV matches. The good friendly staff and quality ale make this ideal for meeting up and planning your visit to London *Imagine a Fullerspoons concept and this would be about it, without the crowds of the big cheap warehouses found elsewhere.* Large and comfortable but retaining the design features that allow for quiet supping, the Mad Bishop and Bear is whatever you want it to be. As a footie fan you might need to dodge the crowds of fellow fans in colours to be allowed through Sushi land to the bar. Alternatively, for London fans going West, catch a breakfast and beer before the train journey out west. Sit on the terrace to get the full interest of being in one of G.W.R.'s beautiful stations.

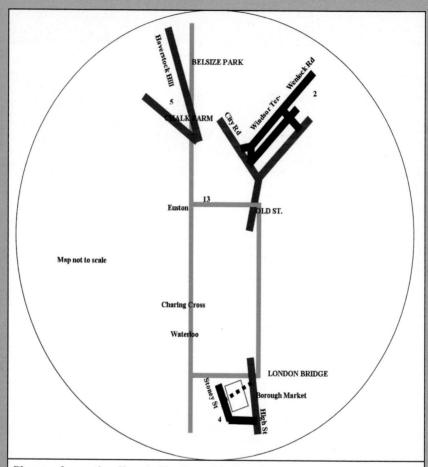

Map not to scale

Changes from other lines to Northern Line

Kings Cross - Victoria, Piccadilly, Hammersmith and City, Metropolitan, Circle and mainline

Tottenham Court Road - Central

Embankment - District

Charing Cross - Bakerloo, Jubilee

Euston - Victoria and mainline

Embankment - Circle, District

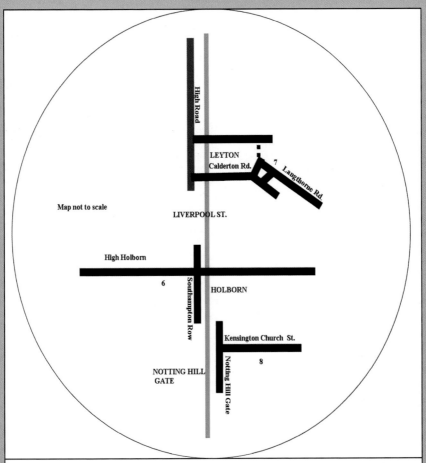

Changes from other lines to Central Line

Holborn - Piccadilly,

Liverpool St - Hammersmith and City, Metropolitan, Circle and mainline

Bank / Monument - Circle, District, Northern, DLR,

Bond St. - Jubilee

Oxford Circus - Bakerloo, Victoria

Notting Hill Gate - Circle, District

London

10 The Dove Fullers

mp   bm

19 Upper Mall, W6 9TA
G Laura and Jim Roff
F From 12
T 020 87485405
S Smoking throughout

BWV 25.1.05 Fullers **London Pride,** Fullers **ESB**

The Dove is a quaint yet modern river side pub with an international reputation. There is a cosmopolitan feel to the pub especially if you join the lunchtime liaison crew and sit on the riverside terrace guessing the many languages of the clientele. Take your partner to impress them with the ale, food, wines or riverside location. My lunchtime visit found several such couples doing the same. It serves seasonal Fullers in addition to the London Pride and ESB. Locals comment that it has *a great relaxing atmosphere in a prime location.* The entrance is in a small mews lane where two wooden, low ceilinged rooms offer farmhouse style drinking. The pub opens out as you venture deeper into the pub, on to a conservatory and then a terrace with views of Hammersmith bridge and associated Thames bustle. I loved the place and it is well worth walking via the underpass from the tube. Even better is to make it an ideal lunchtime finishing point for a Sunday morning urban stroll.

11 Victoria Fullers

mp   tv   bm

10A Stathearn Place, W2 2NH
G Chris Cochran
F Home made traditional pub food from 12
T 020 77241191
S Smoking throughout

BWV 20.12.04 Fullers **ESB Chiswick, London Pride, Jack Frost.**

The pub occupies an imposing street corner location and its reputation is one of a friendly locals pub; it just happens those locals tend to be well off, famous or, as is more often found, long term residents of this more exclusive area of the capital city. It does not however, feel in any way pretentious and is just a great place to drink. It serves excellent Fullers ales to locals who enjoy its peace and quiet. The pub itself is deceptively larger than you first think. It would be my choice for a good lunchtime meal and ale session. Check out the military mantle piece paintings in the bar In this case my visit coincided with an excellent choice of background music, a rarity in pubs nowadays. Music should not, and does not, distract from the core attraction, Fullers ales of high quality in a pub that would be both a local and a destination venue for people visiting the sights of the Paddington area. It is deservedly a Fullers Pub of the year.

12 Carpenter Arms F

mp   sk   bm   pg

12 Seymour Place W1H 7HE
G Sarah Nixon
T 020 77231050
S Smoking throughout.

BWV 20.12.04 Youngs **Winter Warmer, Sussex Bitter**

Just North of Marble Arch and within walking distance of both Paddington and Marylebone the Carpenters Arms is very convenient yet tucked away behind busy Edgware Road. This pub is very comfortable and often busy with Sky sports fans watching on discrete plasma screens. A street corner pub for locals who are working in the area, the client group changes regularly as they move in and out of the area, but students, they are not. On my lunchtime visit I enjoyed settling into the great raised window seats and watching people walking by. At this time of day it is the perfect crossword and pint pub. It is a smaller version of the Market Porter located in a residential rather than Market location. Therefore you get quality rarer guest ales from microbrew rather than those of the ubiquitous London chains. It is at its best as an evening local where the regulars value the normality offered by a proper pub in an area where so often this characteristic is lost in the quest for seemingly quick bucks. Long may this remain so.

13 Head of Steam F 14 Oakdale Arms Freehouse 15 Old Bank Of England

13 Head of Steam F

mp   sk

1 Eversholt St, NW1 2 DN
G Dave O'Sullivan
F From 12
T 020 73833359
S No smoking in upstairs area
W www.theheadofsteam.co.uk

BWV 6.12.04 Banks' **Original**, Dark Star **Porter, Special Edition,** Caledonian **Santa's Little Helper,** Black Sheep **Bitter**, Westons **Vintage Cider**

A station pub as they used to be? No, not cold and draughty, but with railway signs, carriage seating, friendly, helpful staff and a feeling that it's O.K. to miss the train because who wants to rush anyway. The Head of Steam name is spreading but this version still leads the way in creating a real ale club virtually on the station concourse. There are usually up to nine ever changing real ales When planning my journeys home it has always been a place to factor in to travel times, i.e. wherever you are leave time for the HOS before getting the train from Euston. It has one large bar that is creatively split into separate areas and levels. The TVs are very discrete I particularly like to find space in what looks like a mini railway carriage complete with no smoking signs and bench seats so close to each other you can read the paper of your fellow commuter.

14 Oakdale Arms Freehouse

cp   sk   jb   pg

283 Hermitage Rd N4 1NP
G Tom Beran
F Bar food in week and Sunday lunches
T 020 88002013
S Smoking throughout
W www.individualpubs.co.uk

BWV 6.12.04 Grand Union **Autumn Ale**, Milton **Nero, Mammon, Troy**, Nelson **Trafalgar**, Vale **Best Bitter**, Whychert **The Original,** Wadworths **Henry's Original IPA,** Westons **Old Rosie cider**

The Oakdale is a big friendly pub in a striking looking building Guest ales rotate around Milton's regular beers meaning there is always a reward for the real ale hunter, especially fans of microbrew ales.. Once a lager dive Tom has created a loyal and discerning drinkers haven in the traditional style with lounge and public bars. Due to its size it is often busy but rarely crowded. As a real pub it serves locals as much as those who travel distances armed with ale guides. One bar has both pool tables and darts. plus large screens for footie. The slightly larger and grander lounge has space enough for perfectly discrete conversations or sociable chats at the bar. Now CAMRA North London Pub of the Year I vow to return to sample its real ale festival offerings in the summer.

15 Old Bank Of England

mp   bm

194 Fleet St. EC4A 2LJ
G James Carman
F From 12
T 020 74302255
S Separate smoking areas
W Fullers.co.uk

BWV 6.12.04 Fullers **London Pride, ESB Chiswick Bitter, London Porter.**

This must be one of the most well known pubs in the country, the model for the grand ideas of taking large once public historic buildings and creating comfortable and beautiful places to drink. This pub is closed at weekends so we all miss out on what is a national treasure. I therefore, recommend it for evening games. Get there mid afternoon, mingle with the city gents and tourists and marvel at the architecture as you sample Fullers ales at their best. Where to drink in this pub is a bit of a dilemma because there is just too much to take in. Upstairs in the gallery and gaze down on the bustle of the former bank floor?, Around the ornate glazed and panelled bar? Or into one of the stately rooms, often booked by larger groups for meetings? Wherever you choose the effect is just the same, you feel you are part of something quite special. This is the cathedral of the real ale scene yet it is a happy clappy style of worship that you need.

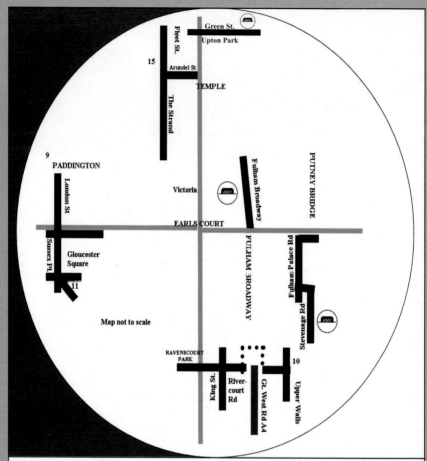

Changes from other lines to District Line,

South Kensington - Piccadilly,

Edgware Rd. - Hammersmith and City, Circle and Bakerloo

Bank / Monument - Circle, District, Northern, DLR,

Victoria - Victoria

Embankment - Bakerloo, District, Circle, Northern

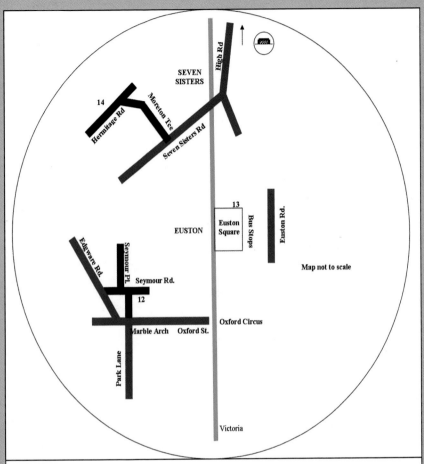

Changes from other lines to Victoria Line,

Finsbury Park - Piccadilly, mainline

Victoria - District, Circle and mainline

Green Park - Jubilee, Piccadilly

Warren St - Northern

Euston - Northern, mainline

Kings Cross - Circle, Hammersmith and City, Northern, Piccadilly, Bakerloo, mainline

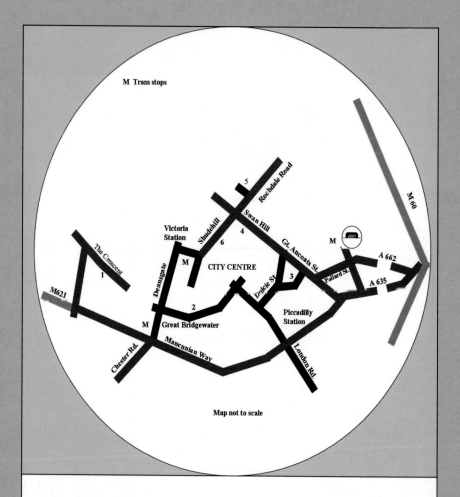

Map not to scale

Manchester City

Manchester has a massive choice of great real ale pubs. Nearer the grounds they change into keg or gastro pubs so my advice is to get into the city centre and use public transport to the ground. My selection tries to give pubs in two areas, Shudehill and Gt. Bridgewater St. with lots of alternatives not mentioned here, plus two more remote, but great pubs, of individual character.

1 The Crescent Freehouse 2 Peveril of the Peak Enterp 3 Jolly Angler Hydes

cp   sk   mp   pg   mp   bm

The Crescent:

18 - 20 The Crescent Salford M3 6AD
G Iris Phillips
T 0161 7365600

BWV **12.3.05** Hydes **Bitter,** Roosters **Special,** Phoenix **Thirsty Moon,** Holdens **Black Country Mild,** Blackwater **Dragon Master,** Northern **Soul Master,** Enville **Womaniser,** Jennings **Golden Host,** Mill St. **Stargazer,** Thatchers **Scrumpy.**

MICROBREW AWARD
The Crescent is my alternative to the town centre route and is included because so many have recommended it. It is one of those places that are hard to leave. During the week the Salford University intelligentsia create a thinking mans drinking den. On evenings and weekends the real ale crew come and go sampling an excellent range of rarer microbrews. It is made up of four very different rooms all with special character. I liked the front bar where the country style fireplace and photos catch the imagination. Football lovers were congregated in the left hand bar sat on sofas and enjoying a critical dissection of all things United. The whole pub has historic timber framed rooms and has a feeling of a Beer Keller complete with European beers. The main attraction is however, the excellent real British beer.

Peveril of the Peak:

127 Gt. Bridgewater St. M1 5JQ
G Maurice Swanick
F from 12
T 0161 2366364
S Separate smoking rooms

BWV **8.06.04** Wychwood **Hobgoblin,** Boddingtons **Bitter,** Charles Wells **Bombardier.**

Oddly shaped and beautifully designed this pub is the place to enjoy pub quirkiness. Bar Football, a mad jukebox and a triangular bar with maximum serving area; all add to the charm of this gem. A place for small groups only as large numbers would soon fill it. *It feels like you could be stepping back into an anachronistic time warp pre war pub. A good selection of real ales is available and are always in immaculate condition. (Beer advocate)* The other advantage is that The Peveril of the Peak is the most traditional of real ale houses in an area full of alternatives. *It is in total contrast to the nearby and excellent Rain Bar.* Similarly the open welcome for footie and ale fans contrasts with the welcome you might receive in other local pubs. On Manchester United days the pub will be heaving so my advice is to make it part of a city day or a weekend away visit. You cannot miss the pub, just look out for the tiles on the outside, the heritage status is plainly obvious.

Jolly Angler:

47 Ducie St, M1 2JW
G Sheila Reynolds
T 0161 2365307
S Smoking throughout

BWV18.06.04 Hydes **Bitter, Anvil.**

Meet with Man City fans here before going to watch your team at United, You will love it for the craic. I arrived at opening time one evening, it quickly filled up with regulars who freely advised me to stay rather than go for another beer elsewhere, *it is well worth it because the music starts soon.* It has *great Irish music sessions* An hour later I had trouble squeezing past the throng to get out and the fiddles and bows had yet to start up. The locals said to *go there to meet Joey Ramone behind the bar.* The chat had been great, the Mickey taking cruel and *a pub to remember* committed to my mind. It may have a very limited Hydes beer option but it is an essential part of the Manchester experience. The Jolly Angler is the joker in the Manchester pack, on the pub door it said *This toilet is for the use of pub patrons only.* The reality is this pub is open to all and will guarantee a fine welcome. Its walls declare allegiance to Man City players new and old. The beer represents the traditions of Manchester ales fast being lost.

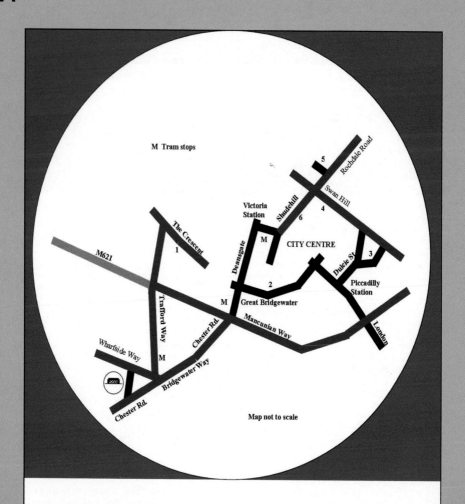

Manchester United

Manchester has a massive choice of great real ale pubs. Nearer the grounds they change into keg or gastro pubs so my advice is to get into the city centre and use public transport to the ground. My selection tries to give pubs in two areas, Shudehill and Gt. Bridgewater St. with lots of alternatives not mentioned here, plus two more remote, but great pubs, of individual character.

4 Smithfield Hotel and Bar Fr

5 The Beer House Freehouse

6 Hare and Hounds Punch

mp sk

37 Swan St,M4 5JZ
G Jennifer Poole
T 0161 839 4424
S Smoking throughout

BWV 18.12.04 Robinsons **Dark Hatter,** Fullers **Jack Frost,** Lodden **Razzle Dazzle,** Oakham **Gravity,** Chimera **Winter Weasel,** Phoenix **Smithfield**.

This is a long narrow bar that manages to satisfy a wide range of real ale hunters. The landlady has a deservedly good reputation for quality ales that are different to the local norm. It will get crowded but seating soon becomes available as crawlers come and go. As Beerin-theevening says *Overall an excellent pub and a must for real ale drinkers. Prices? about £1.80 for a pint of something you've never heard of A must on the M4 beer run*. My visit was part of a footie away weekend and with cheap accommodation both here and in nearby guest houses you find that Manchester is a great location for a large number of teams. (I would have liked to stay here, in my case for a Rochdale away game). Places are often taken by real ale trekkers basing themselves in the Shudehill area. The great attraction is as always the choice of ever changing guest ales and the warm, faintly old fashioned, company you find here.

mp   bm

6 Angel Street, M4 4BR
G Paul Higginson
F From 12
T 0161 8397019
S Smoking throughout

BWV 18.12.04 Brains **SA,** Beerhouse **Premium,** Black Sheep **Bitter,** Moorhouses **Black Cat,** Riches **Cider,** Westons **Perry,** St. Austell **HSD,** Cains **FA,** Pictish **Celtic Warrior,** Leadmill **William IV ESM,** Archers **Golden**

On my visit it was noisy and very friendly with a fantastic range of ales. Everyone was commenting on how good the beer was; very unusual when the range is so wide. This pub has a refreshingly simple charm sorely long lost in so many pubs. *The Beer House is just what its name describes - a top place in Manchester to try new kinds of beer.* The regulars range from pub crawlers doing the Shudehill circuit, professional beer tickers sampling new ales and regulars using this pub as the best place for good chat and ale. My visits coincided on both occasions with an impromptu party going on among the more youthful elements of the clientele. It is a proper unorganised fun pub, a mates pub, a beer and cider lovers pub, most of all a lively pub, not one to bring your programme and hope to read it.

mp sk   bm   pg   d

Shudehill M 4 4AA
G Max Doyle
F Sandwiches at the bar plus pickled eggs and onions
T 0161 8349088
S No Smoking at the bar

BWV 12.3.05 Holts **Bitter,** Tetley's **Bitter.**

The Hare and Hounds has national historical importance and a chance to get top quality Holts in great surroundings. Max describes her pub *as a mans pub* yet it will be a great place for the early evening pint before the cinema or in a place to chill out before a metro ride to the game. It is very much a regulars s pub, it just happens they come from a wider area than usual. Mark of London enthuses as he says *the banter is always good humoured, the atmosphere congenial, and the beer is always spot on!* The many visitors marvel at the 1930's refurbishment complete with Tube station style tiling and glass screens. Tony of Manchester sums it up as *a massive Man City pub, brill T.V. for football games and a great landlady and staff.* Pat reassuringly says *its not only City and United they support, it's the game of football.* I would need to be convinced however, to join in the passion for eggs and pickles either before or after a game. This is one of my award winning pubs.

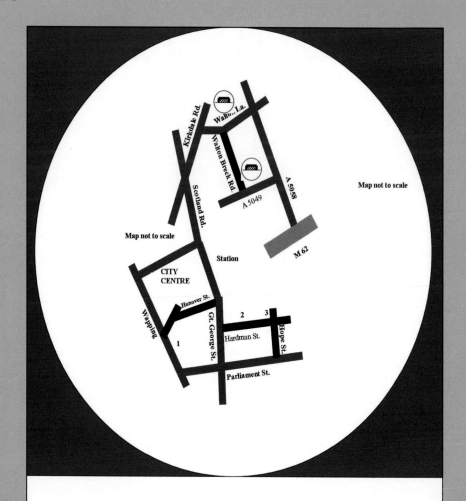

Liverpool Central and South

These choices represent a mini crawl in the more touristy parts of Liverpool focusing on the Cathedrals and Quayside to the south of the City Centre. Probably better done by taxi, many will want to get into the newly redeveloped port with its bars and museums. The Hope St. area has several good alternatives to those in this guide.

Liverpool

1 Baltic Fleet Wapping Beers

2 Fly in the Loaf O'Kells

3 The Philharmonic M+B

sp   bm

33 A Wapping L1 8DQ
G Gary Wright and Richard Peel
F Modern British food
T 0151 7093116
S Separate smoking areas

BWV 28.2.05 Wapping **Brunel, Bow Spirit Bitter, Summer Ale, Tapley Mild,** Tigertops **Right Rye.**

Wapping beers are a personal favourite of mine and to go to their home was a particular treat that didn't disappoint. The pub is an impressive island among the redeveloped hotels and car parks along the dockland highway. The scale of the pub is delightfully appropriate. One smaller bar is festooned with superb photos of dockside scenes. The longer second bar is on a different level and arranged cafe style for larger groups to sit around tables and then an upstairs eating area gives more space when needed. Large windows give glimpses of the Liver building and Cathedral, most visitors will, however, concentrate on the excellent range of ales plus ever changing guests. The Baltic Fleet has won numerous awards and it is easy to see this as a destination pub. If you only have time to visit one pub in Liverpool then this grade II listed building and brewery would make the perfect choice. Without doubt *mines a Wapping one.* Of Course it is .

mp sk   bm   d

Hardman St. L1 9AS
G Dominic Hornsby
F Full menu available 7 days a week 12 - 6.45
T 0151 7080817
S Smoking policy to be decided

BWV Oakham **JHB**, Cottage **Peregrine,** Wickwar **Right Flanker,** Pardoes **Bumblehole,** O'Kells **McLair, IPA, Bitter.**

This is the newest kid on the real ale block and has all the qualities of the nearby Dispensary. This converted bakehouse has references to its history within the large freeze slogans. This is where the concessions to the past end.. I will confess to liking the real air of confidence in the pub. It is great to sample O'Kells brews in a room that offers a range of drinking spaces. I preferred to catch up on the large screen T.V. while Laura and her brother Phil wanted to check out the newer guests on offer. It was all very friendly and a slap in the face to large style city pubs, It is a pub rather than a cheap drinking space, *with service that is efficient, friendly and knowledgeable (Colin of Liverpool)* and long may this continue. Nothing, however, could console the Liverpool fans recovering from the Cup Final defeat of the previous day. It does for some, *make going to the match a close call .*

mp   bm

36 Hope St. L1 9BX
G Marie Louise Wong
F From 12
T 0151 709 1163
S Separate smoking areas

BWV 28.2.05 Ridleys **Old Bob,** Shepherd Neame **Spitfire,** Batemans **Hopbine Bitter,** Green King **Old Speckled Hen,** Cains **Bitter.**

Onwards and upwards to the Philharmonic and what a climb up in terms of grandeur. Described by Egon Ronay as the most ornate pub in Britain I would prefer the qualities of gob smacking, jaw dropping stateliness. The Grand Lounge must be unique in its scale. The other drawing rooms ooze comfort and history. Not solely the preserve of concert goers, the pub is of national importance and we are so lucky that beer quality attempts to reach the unattainable standards of the building. And then there are the toilets, what is this an architectural guide? Well I'm sorry it has to be done. The beer was very good, guest ales rotating about the regular Cains and Deuchars. IPA. My evening visit found a wide variety of customers, couples enjoying the cosiness of the smaller rooms, large groups meeting mates in the Grand lounge, I joined those who wanted a relaxing post work pint at the bar. Excellent!

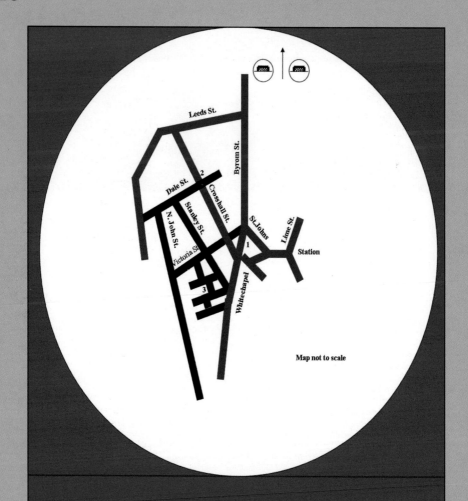

Map not to scale

Liverpool Central and North

This is a grand real ale City with a legacy that ranges from modern reconstructions to Victorian grandeur that rivals any British examples. There are many fine hostelries not included here so a walking tour between these pubs will find others to supplement this fantastic ale selection. The un reviewed Strawberry Tavern also lies nearer the ground. Happy hunting, you can't fail to do well here.

Liverpool

1 Dr. Duncan's Cains   **2 Ship and Mitre** Freehouse   **3 White Star** Enterprise

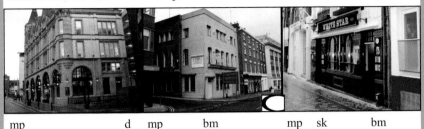

mp   d   mp   bm   mp   sk   bm

St. Johns House, St. Johns St. L1 1HF
G Peter Howarth
T From 12 Mon. to Friday only.
T 0151 7095100
S Smoking throughout
W www.cainsbeers.com

BWV 28.2.05 Cains **Bitter, IPA, Dark Mild, 2008** Victorian Ale, Addlestones **Cloudy Cider,** Orkney **Raven Ale,** Wychwood **Wolf Rider.**

The good Doctors pub is not as large as one might think on first observation. The corner public bar is a gem, Ornate tiled pillars in the Victorian splendour. The other public bar is a good chatting area with original seating facing the traffic through picture windows. The rear of the pub is a spilt level lounge, less grand but equally comfortable. Most impressive, however, is the variety of Cains ales supplemented by a good choice of guest ales. This place is a regular award winner and the conversation appeared very footie orientated. I would imagine, due to its proximity to Lime Street Station, it to be very busy most days and on Saturdays in particular. A great starting point for a visit to this fine ale town. In my case it was the regular afternoon shift that filled the bars with a constant purr of contentment enjoying different beers from their last visit.

133 Dale St. L2 2HJ
G Brian Corrin
F From 12 (not Sat.)
T 0151 2360859
S Smoking throughout
W www.shipandmitre.com

BWV 28.2.05 Weetwood **Ambush,** Burton Bridge **Stairway to Heaven,** Ossett **Ellens Glory,** Slaters **Premium,** Durham **White Gold,** Wentworth **Oatmeal Stout,** Salopian **Shropshire Gold,** Cottage **Broadgauge.**

My town centre award pub rapidly came to be my personal Liverpool favourite due in no small part to the great welcome of the locals. Joe, the Everton fan outlined just how great this pub is on match days, *good friendly banter, shared lifts in taxis etc* and it sounds just perfect. Add in the recommendations from those in the other pubs in this guide page and you should have no doubt that the Ship and Mitre is the Gold Standard of Liverpool real ale pubs. The design is apparently of a ship galley. I was reminded more of a Scandinavian sauna, pine clad bar with larger more American diner style lounge design to the rear. One can only dream of my team getting to play in town and take up the offer of the good time to be had. Perhaps it will be a beer festival visit. Cheers Joe.

2-4 Rainford Gardens (Off Matthew St.) L12 6PT
G Alfie Buxton
T 0151 2316861
S Smoking throughout
W www.thewhitestar.co.uk

BWV 28.2.05 **Bass.**Caledonian **Deuchars IPA,** Bowland **Hunters Moon, Nicky Nook, White Star Pale Ale, 1745,**

Alfie and the White Star are something of Liverpool legends. It is easy to wax lyrical about the back room with its genuine Beatles connections, or rave on about the Boxing memorabilia that includes Cooper and Ali stuff. The real draw for me was the chance to get Bowland Beer and also to check out the history of the Czech Republic connections. Having been at the Euro 96 games and witnessed the Czech friendliness at first hand it says a lot of the pub that this continues to the present day. To find it you need to follow the signs to the Cavern area and then follow the real ale tickers, perhaps carrying this guide, to the pub. Once there you will find it difficult to move on as the list of ales is both interesting and novel. When I visited the pub was perfectly unaffected by the tourists strolling nearby. A great retreat in the middle of tourist land, I would want to visit here whenever possible.

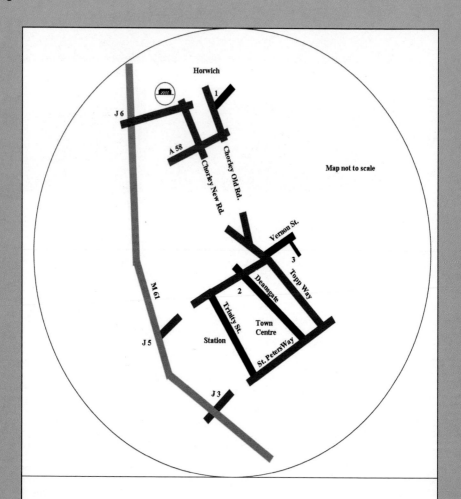

Horwich

J 6

A 58

Chorley Old Rd.

Chorley New Rd.

1

Map not to scale

Vernon St.

3

Deansgate

Topp Way

M 61

2

Trinity St.

Town Centre

J 5

Station

St. Peters Way

J 3

Bolton

The home of the Bank Top Brewery and Howcroft Beer festival will not disappoint. The Reebok's location means that much many seek ale in Horwich and Westhoughton. It would be a shame however, not to sample the quality found in town or high on the hill.

1 Bob's Smithy Freehouse 2 Hen and Chickens Punch 3 Howcroft Inn Punch

cp   bm   mp   tv   bm   cp   sk   pg   d

1488 Chorley Old Rd BL1 7GX
G Stuart Brooks
T 01204 842622
S Smoking throughout.

BWV 1.3.05 Timothy Taylor **Landlord**, Tetley's **Bitter**, Tetley's **Mild,** Archers **Golden Orchard**, Boddingtons **Bitter.** Bank top **Flat Cap Bitter**

High, at the end of the Old Chorley Road, Bob's Smithy comes as the resting place for the tired and weary. Another 200m takes you to the brow of the hill and a view across the valley to the silhouette of the Reebok *Trainer-dome*. This is a true country pub, family run and wonderfully not a restaurant or theme park pub, it is a proper pub. Stone walled outside, carpeted within and with typical country inn decoration this pub is very cosy, log fires and all. Trotters from across the Metropolitan area often meet here with the more adventurous away fans to marvel at the ease of which the moors become accessible to town up here. As a southern softie it is a car ride for me to the ground (2 miles or so) and a resolution to return after a long walk in summer when I could make good use of the outside benches with one of the guest ales which always includes something from the local Bank top Brewery, this factor alone making it worth a visit.

143 Deansgate BL1 1EX
G Anthony and Hilary Coyne
F Full menu from 11.30 -2 Mon. to Sat
T 01204 389836
S Separate no smoking areas at lunchtimes only

BWV1.3.05 Greene King **Old Speckled Hen**, Kelham **Pale Island**, Wadworths **JCB,** Tetley's **Bitter**, Cains **Mild.**

This pub has variety and cosiness to spare. There are lots of places to hide away with a programme or beer guide or as the locals do, gather around the bar and engage in cross bar "Cheers style" conversation. The pub is a bit of a Bolton legend, having a range of guests that enrich the diet of national staples. I loved the room nearest the bar especially the photos and shirt of Wynn Davies alongside Wanderers memorabilia. There are also many references to Bolton's role in the charge of the light brigade. Why do Bolton play so often on Sundays? Nothing to do with Sky, just that the Hen and Chickens isn't open so the gathering of the Trotters wouldn't then be possible. So it becomes a recommendation for a stop off in the town centre for those using the train to the town centre. The locals hold this place in spotless reverence, visitors love the genuine Bolton welcome.

36 Pool St BL1 2
G Clive Nightingale
F Pub grub before the game 12 - 2 (5 Sundays) snacks and wholesome meals with home cooked chips.
T 01204 526814
S Smoking throughout

BWV 1.3.05, Bank Top **Golden Digger**, Tetley's **Bitter,** Timothy Taylor **Landlord**, Rudgate **Battle Axe.**

Holding a legendary status among those who offered suggestions to this guide the Howcroft is a pub to cherish. Surrounded by a wall of new houses the pub has a bowling green to add to the timber framed and glass partitioned snugs and vaults that lead away from the central bar. Clive has fame as a landlord through the October, Howcroft beer festival that raises shed loads for charity and champions the work of Micro brews and independents. The pub draws its regulars from larger than normal distances and include corporate evenings, sampling ale and bowls. My visit found them in inevitable conversation about beer and left me wondering whether I should extend my recommendations to Clive's other pub, the Hope and Anchor, along the Chorley Old Road to Horwich from Bolton. This is my award winning local.

THE PERFECT FOOTBALL AND

This article is a bit of unashamed self indulgence where I attempt to describe the perfect footie and real trip by drawing on examples from the year spent travelling the country researching these guides.

My perfect day starts the day before when I arrive in town armed with a mental list of pubs to check out on a Friday evening pub crawl. I say the night before because the perfect town deserves more than a cursory sampling of one or two pubs. Arriving the night before avoids that horrible feeling of finding the wrong pub on the match day through lack of preparation.

My perfect Friday night in the Premiership would be spent in **Newcastle.** Check out the **Crown Posada,**

others should be in the guide. The best fun is found by being led by the advice of the locals. They will know the unrecognised new ale outlets or those under new management and deserving of some publicity. One such piece of advice found me going from **Dr. Duncan's** to my perfect new find of the year the **Fly in the Loaf Liverpool**

No Friday night would be perfect unless it involved meeting up with like minded away fans to compare notes, have a meal or share a curry after closing. The pub needs to have space for a large group to sit together, therefore being quieter than the typical town centre clubbers pub. In the case of the **Hare and Hounds**

The View from the Free Trade, Newcastle

The Fly in the Loaf

too small and crowded for a pre match pint for me yet brilliant the night before. Then stroll around the city centre before heading off to Byker on the metro for a crawl on the riverside and great company, live music and Mordue ales.

I have designed the guide to allow for those who also like finding other real ale pubs. I would dip in and out, making a mental note to canvass the views of my friends as to whether

in Manchester you have the added bonus of a beautiful location and a landlady who knows that tourists make up a fair number of drinkers, yet still generates a regulars pub feel right in the middle of the city. I would therefore end my real ale evening among friends and locals, sampling a local ale.

Breakfast and beer? Well why not. You could try a pub in a city market like the **Market Porter in London.**

REAL ALE TRIP - PREMIERSHIP

My choice would involve a later start and a railway station often offers some great possibilities. My perfect railway station location would take me to the **Mad Bishop and Bear** at Paddington. Spacious, relaxing and offering quality Fullers ales it is perfect for sitting over a paper and planning the day ahead.

Having done my research the night before I would then meet up with locals who support their team in one of the pubs I visited the previous evening. The pub will often be some distance from the ground, perhaps on a bus or tram route. Ideally I would arrange to meet mates from my team who have travelled up on the day. As they enjoy the joyous variety that of a lunch time beer and chat before a game. Masses of real ale then is the order of the day, perhaps the **Fat Cat in Norwich**, or the **Bartons Arms in Birmingham** but my perfect pre match pub would be the **Kelham Island Tavern in Sheffield**. Not in the Premiership I know but everything is not always best at the top and sometimes we have things better outside the top division.

Then, unfortunately for me, its off to the game. Afterwards no doubt drowning my sorrows comes into play. There will be more pubs to find, friends to seek consolation in, a train to catch. Programme in hand, it will be perfect to return to a nearby local, or into town for a final ale.

Mad Bishop and Bear

Kelham Island Tavern

real ale should offer, perhaps a dark beer for myself, a real cider for the west country faithful or a full bodied local brew for the guys who look for a quick alcohol effect. The pub should provide something different but it must feel comfortable for home and away fans. No Burberry clad Muppets will be found in my choice. I love to mix in with the fans who bring their wives and children with them, maintaining the traditions So for me it would be somewhere like the **Ship and Mitre in Liverpool,** the crowds of earlier may have gone yet the beer will be constant, the atmosphere good and the station or bed and breakfast nearby. Joe the Everton fan will have been good company at lunchtime but now it is time to recharge the batteries and plan for next weekend. Happy hunting!

Stedders 2005

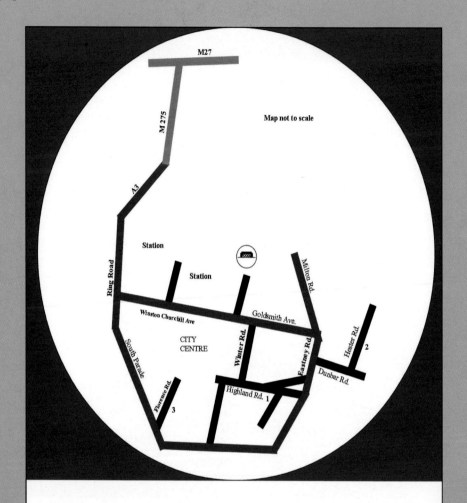

Portsmouth

Portsmouth sprawls and as a result the real ale hunt involves large distances if you want to sample all on offer. Unlike most seaside towns there is plenty on offer. My recommendation sends you to Eastney where the pubs will be crowded on matchdays but the welcome friendlier than nearer the ground. For those who can't resist the sea then the Florence is a welcome retreat.

Portsmouth

1 Sir Loin of Beef Freehouse   **2 Artillery Arms** Freehouse   **3 Florence Arms** Roundabout

sp   jb   d   sp   sk   sp   tv   bm   pg

152 Highland Rd, PO4 9NH
G Paul Jevons
T 07766646972 / 023 92820115

BWV 9.2.05 Courage **Directors,** Hampshire **Heaven Can Wait,** Hall and Woodhouse **Slurpin Santa,** Haddas **Head Banger,** Gales **HSB,** Ruddles **County,** Hopback **Summer Lightning, GHB, Stowford Press Cider.**

When seen from the outside this pub has the appearance of a cheerful seaside street corner café. On entry, you soon know you are in serious real ale land. It is *rated by PubzOnline as the best pub in Pompey* and has a loyal band of Pompey advocates I particularly liked the attempts to find originality in the design and layout though I just couldn't sit on the Carling bench. I would be tempted by the bottle list and on occasions the Gales wines always issue a challenge. The beer range, however, is the main attraction here along with the options to just sit and watch the locals' obvious good fortune. Top beer and a landlord who organises beer trips to the many Hampshire breweries for the regulars, that is what I call looking after my customers. It is a good 10 minute walk to the ground, far enough away to avoid the masses, close enough to get full value making it my close to ground award winner.

Hester Rd, Eastney PO4 8HB
G Mike and Annette Bradshaw
F From 12
T 023 9273 3610

BWV 9.2.05 Gales **HSB,Bitter, Cheriton Pots Ale** Ringwood **Old Thumper, Forty Niner,** , Itchen Valley **Gold Ale,** Archers **Springboard.**

This is a large back street boozer with a difference. Home of the Pompey anoraks on matchdays it is geared up to sports lovers of all types. Recommended by many away fans *for the friendly welcome* the Artillery always has the Ringwood and Gales options plus guests from local breweries. Mike tells me that the refurbishments likely will not change the character. To do so would be to remove the proper pub features that are loved by locals and visitors alike. He also wants to continue the links with the Pompey past, they are everywhere in the hanging flags, newspaper cuttings but mostly in the friendly fans who frequent this top boozer. I chose the small bar on the street entrance side, smaller and more chatty than the larger rooms that held space for events and pub games. The award is partly due to the not so friendly nature of pubs elsewhere in Portsmouth. The Artillery has a welcome all would cherish, another award winner.

18 - 20 Florence Rd, Southsea PO5 2NE
G Jane Goldring and Greg Clark
F Not on matchdays
T 023 92875700

BWV 9.2.05 Youngs **Bitter, Special.** Addlestsones **Cider,** Adnams **Broadside,**

This pub is perfect for the family / couples and real ale strollers who enjoy a walk on the seafront as part of the match day routine. Come inland a couple of minutes and you will find the Florence. It has a certain confident style having been refurbished in what appears to be an interesting mix of styles. The bars offer the option of modern style, all pine floors etc. or traditional décor with dark wooden timber furniture and pub games.. Alas my midweek visit missed the locals' choice of guest ales which is available at the weekend. On Saturday food is not available because the separate rear room restaurant is transformed into the favoured meeting place for Pompey fans from afar. It gets very busy because Pompey fans meet here after quite distant journeys back home. Greg is a top landlord who makes you feel welcome and serves top quality Youngs ales. The alternatives are from a range of guest ales, usually regional or local speciality beers.

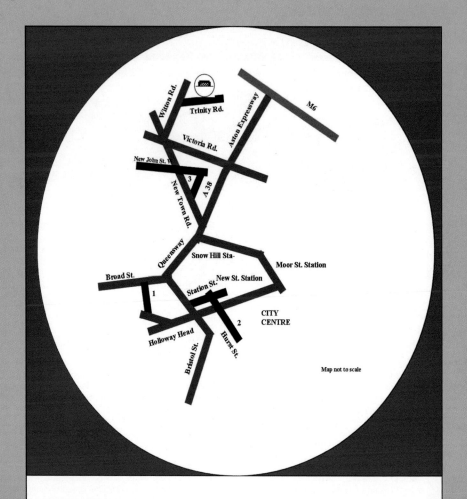

Map not to scale

Aston Villa

Villa fans tend to find pubs near to the ground in the City centre itself so this guide entry concentrates on a selection of pubs a bit further away but in easy walk of the three stations. The Bartons Arms is the jewel in this particular Crown.

Birmingham

1 City Tavern Freehouse

2 Old Fox Independent

3 Bartons Arms Freehouse

| mp sk bm pg | mp bm | sp tv bm d |

38 Bishopsgate B15 1EJ
G Vicki Banks
F Pub food from 12
T 0121 6438467
S Smoking throughout

54 Hurst St B5 4TD
G Gerry Poutney
F From 12
T 0121 622 5080
S Smoking throughout

144 High St Aston B6 4UP
G Changed since visit
F Thai food from12
T 0121 3335988
S Separate smoking areas
W www.bartons-arms.co.uk

BWV 20.2.05 Highgate **Dark Mild**, **Special**, Hook Norton **Old Hooky**, Highwood **Tom Woods Old Timber**, St Austell **Tribute**.

This is the real ale answer to what is going on in nearby Broad Street While the bright lights shine around the corner the City Tavern draws the faithful with a mix of great ale and music. At lunchtimes the discerning office worker seeks it out for a touch of reality. In the evening this Grade II Victorian listed building gives way to a wide range of traditional music. The reputation for fun also involves good live music and story telling sessions held upstairs. It has managed to keep (or salvage) much of its original Victorian furniture when Highgate Brewery saved the pub from oblivion. It relies on people who seek good, ale, good pub grub and good conversation. It is a lively place but in the friendly relaxed way. It also features large screen Sky T.V. for those who wander in from nearby trendy dwellings of the Five Ways / Gas Street area. It would have been easy to spoil this place by pandering to lager and gastro pub fans.

BWV 20.2.05 ,Greene King **Old Speckled Hen**, Marstons **Pedigree**, Tetley **Bitter**, Everards **Tiger**, **Tiger Gold**, Hanby **Coopers Pride**, Church End **Vicars Ruin**, Everards **Sunchaser**.

In the Theatre district / Chinatown this pub is popular with those who need quick service between acts. I, however, wouldn't rush as the choice of beers offers something for the person who seeks a difference. You can expect to find unusual local microbrews and seasonal ales, well served in an atmosphere that is sophisticated yet personable. It is very handy for the City centre but the place is a magnet in its own right. The Hurst street I remember is much changed but retains its atmosphere as a place where students and antipodeans congregate to enjoy the street life. The Old Fox has a prominent location and gets very busy on those lazy summers days when all you need is good company and people to share your choice of ales. I would enjoy the company of a group of friends here, watch others watching others and perhaps lay into a Chinese meal to follow.

BWV 20.2.05 Breconshire **Winter Beacon**, Mauldons **Eatanswill Old**, Nethergate **Umbel Ale**, Oakham **JHB**, **Bishops Farewell**.

To some pubs are like Churches. If so then the Bartons is a Cathedral. A Grade II listed Victorian Classic it can be seen well before you are close. Once inside I spent much time raising my eyes to spot another glory in the building. The beer is chosen in the style of other Oakham pubs with quality microbrews as well as home ales. It is easy to find, too easy, but you won't notice the masses of other people here on match days. Well perhaps I've lost it now, but you get the idea. And I haven't even got to the Thai Food. Oakham breweries have a knack of creating great ale houses across the country. My visit became a rather longer session than I envisaged because there seemed to be just another beer that needed to be sampled and the locals wanted to chat footie in general and Villa in particular. Come again after the game and let the traffic clear itself before venturing home.

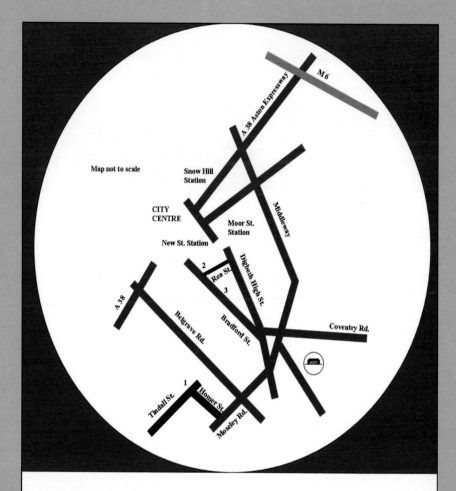

Birmingham

It is a long drag out from the City Centre to St. Andrews. Near the ground you are advised not to have a quiet beer as you won't easily find one, quiet that is. The pubs here are good old fashioned boozers that will be heaving on matchdays but well worth a visit on other days should you find time or the inclination to visit again

Birmingham

1 Old Moseley Arms Punch

2 Anchor Freehouse

3 White Swan W+D

sp	tv	bm	pg

mp	sk	bm	pg

mp	sk	bm

1 Old Moseley Arms

Tindal St, B12 9QU
G Sukhi Rai
F Curries Tue and Thu evenings
T 0121 4401954
S Smoking throughout

BWV 21 2.05, Enville **Ale, Ginger,** Black Sheep **Bitter,** Greene King **Abbot.**

A boozer from the top drawer. My Sunday evening visit was very busy as the T.V. footie watching boozers gave way to the regulars coming from a not so local area to enjoy the obvious good company found here. The bars are very different. I sat in, and preferred the smaller cosier brick walled bar while others spread themselves out in the larger, darker lounge. For me it was a taxi fare well spent, the choice of ale is good and well served by friendly bar staff. The food has a good reputation among those telling me about the pub. I might return to try out the upstairs pool room or the Tuesday or Thursday night curry. More likely I can see this as very handy for the Edgbaston test. Roll on the summer. The pub runs its own cricket teams and is reputedly one of those impromptu music haunts. The Old Mo is actually in Balsall Heath but has the feel of a Moseley sets local, also catering for immediate locals and their regular community needs.

2 Anchor

308 Bradford St. B5 6ET
G Dean Pursell
F From 12
T 0121 6224516
S Separate no smoking bar
W www.the-anchor-inn.fsnet.co.uk

BWV 20.2.05 Hanby **Coopers Mild,** Wye Valley **White Knuckle,** Skinners **Tinners,** Cheddar Valley **Traditional Cider,** Greene King **Abbot,** Hambleton **Nightmare,** Brown Cow **Old E'ter,** Beartown **Pandamonium,** Roosters **Brewers Gold,** Cannon Royale **Arrowhead,** Foxield **White Fox.**

Pub of the Year awards are celebrated here as the tradition for top quality ale continues to draw those venturing just beyond the new Bull Ring or arriving via Digbeth Coach Station. My visit was entertaining as the locals played pool much to the mirth of the new visitors. It has a cosmopolitan feel, has a certain earthy quality and is certainly one that the real ale fan will recognise as putting the ale at the top of the priority order, no flowery wallpaper here. What you do get is a genuine welcome and a great atmosphere on matchdays. Local CAMRA pub of the year most years because the choice of ales is remarkable and the quality consistently good. There are no regular ales, just a constant surprise as ales rotate endlessly.

3 White Swan

276 Bradford St B12 0QY
G Agnes Cretton
F From 12
T 0121 6222586
S Smoking throughout

BWV 20.2.05 Banks' **Original, Bitter, Mild.**

This is cracking pub. A place where the architecture adds interest but doesn't distract from the serious beer reveling. Spot the similarities with the photo of the Bartons Arms. While I watched the Sky T.V. brand soccer the locals were readily willing to chat about beer, sport in general and just how good this pub is. There is a genuine Irish angle to the entertainment on offer. It is also heaving on matchdays so get there early, not in colours because while the locals will make you more than welcome, the others on Bradford St. may be less generous in their greetings. I loved this pub and would visit whenever in town. Perhaps next time it with a Rugby international for the Landlord certainly looks after those locals, they were last heard planning the annual trip to watch the Irish, this time in Paris. Several beers later I forced myself with some reluctance to leave the comfort of my corner seat in the White Swan to check out the less attractive City Centre trendy ale houses.

THE COMPETITION FOR

I would like to thank the 400 or so people who contributed to the guides by completing the post cards given to them by landlords in the pubs.

The aim was to give the writing a more personalised set of descriptions by asking people who know the pubs best to comment on the good points that make their locals so good.

to visit both this year and next. It also confirmed my view that the beauty of finding good real ale is that the country has many real ale outlets that are as yet given their true worth of advertising. Some of the entries did not serve real ale put are still great footie pubs.

The comments were many and varied and some unfortunately unprint-

Geoff Clarke, (left) the winner of the competition pictured with "Pat" Patel, the landlord of the Old Crown in West Bromwich (right) and the owner of the Malvern Brewery on a recent trip organised by Pat. We wish Pat a full recovery from his recent illness and look forward to Geoff enjoying his two tickets to an away game next season.

Many comments were used in the guide and they can be seen it italics in many entries. Wherever possible I have tried to give the name that the contributor wished to use. If the person wished to remain anonymous the quotation remains without a name rather than as anon.

I also asked the entrants to nominate their best away footie fan pub in the country. This was a very interesting exercise which threw up many pubs for me

able. Without doubt those places that returned cards ended up with a more interesting entry that reflected the humour found in those pubs. The vast majority of comments were a great help in giving me their true flavour beyond that which can be made in my short visits,

From the entries I selected eleven finalists. These cards were the most interesting, funny or informative. The finalists are listed opposite

My personal favourite was from

CONTRIBUTORS TO THE GUIDE

Dawn of West Bromwich who said the Wheatsheaf is handy for the baggies matches as it's *between the Doctors surgery and the church.* I am writing this just as the Baggies have survived for another year. Someone certainly prayed a lot this afternoon.

The draw was held in a London pub on the night of a Conference play off semi final. Pictured here are Clarkie, Tim, Kelly and Graham, surveying the finalists before selecting a winner. The finalists were selected as the most interesting entered, the winner was a random selection from that list.

FINALISTS

Geoff Clarke	Wednesbury
Mike Stevens,	Dudley,
Gary S	Barnsley
Phil Passingham	Market Harborough
Dawn	West Bromwich
Nicola S	Barnsley
Mark	London
Jean Downey	Sunderland
Steve	Luton
David Cuff	Brighton
Dave Knight	Brighton

Geoff's entry for the Old Crown (West Bromwich) said *Not only is it a baggies base we also have Villa, Blues, Wolves and Walsall supporters and the rapport is fantastic - almost as good as the real ale (Always varying in type but never in quality. The best value food in Sandwell and by far the most accommodating host and hostess.*

He also recommended the Black Eagle in Hockley as a Walsall fan.

Good luck if you enter next years competition. I look forward to your entries.

Stedders 2005

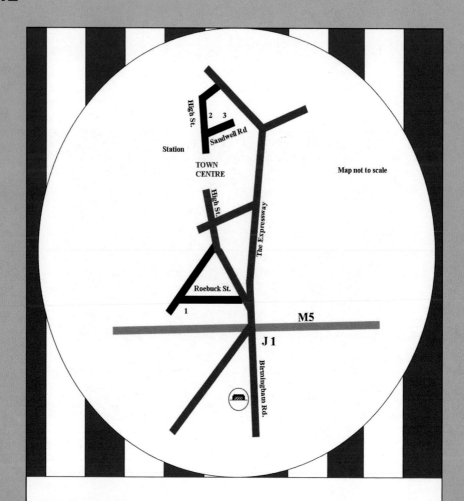

West Bromwich

As everyone knows The Hawthorns is in Sandwell and separated from its town centre by the M6. It is however well connected by the metro service and my recommendations find three very different ale houses that have good footie and real ale reputations that should be cherished. It is no coincidence that these pubs are sought by fans looking for a touch of quality and something a bit different.

West Bromwich

1 The Vine Freehouse   2 Wheatsheaf Holden's   3 Old Crown Freehouse

sp	sk	bm		d	sp	tv	bm	pg	d	sp	sk	d

152 Roebuck St, B70 6RD
G Suki Patel
F Tandoori bar-b-que and speciality curries and baltis, pub grub.
T 0121 5532866
S Smoking may be separate
W www.thevine.co.uk

BWV 22.2.05 Bathams Bitter.

On my many visits to this ground breaking pub the atmosphere has always been the same. Crowded, and lively it has a *great atmosphere, friendly staff, good real ale selection (Adam of C Heath)* It has been extended, extended and extended again so that the original bar is tiny compared to the series of canteen style dining spaces that stretch it seems back as far as the nearby M5. Mark says *that if you can be happy after watching the baggies there must be something in the beer.* The single real ale is always changing so the choice is as surprising as the food is cheap and good. *Away supporters are welcomed (Chris Whitehouse) and where else would you find so many footie experts (Rose of Sedgeley)* Suki makes a great effort to make the casual visitor as welcome as the regular Baggies who swamp this pub on matchdays. Get there early if you want a seat. And of course as Marie says, *Deb works here.* Patrons *leave with red hands, this is my food award winner.*

379 High St.B70 3QW
G Dave Forrest
F Pork stuffing crusty, chips, sandwiches, main meals, Chillie and gammon.
T 0121 5534221
S Smoking unknown
W www.thewheatsheaf@supernet.com

BWV 22.2.05 Holden's **Bitter, Special, Passionate Monk, Golden Glow.**

The Wheatsheaf is located *between the doctors surgery and the church, handy for Baggies fans. (Dawn of West Bromwich)* The Holden's beer is the major attraction especially as Dave serves a good range that suits most tastes and it was very good. The pub has been extended to the rear and the lounge has a stately home feel. I preferred the smaller front bar, like a market town tap room and the best bet for chat with the locals and footie fans. On non match days take a paper and do as the regulars do, relax, chill out and drink Holden's by numbers. For example Mike Stevens of Dudley waxes, b*efore the Baggies game I get a golden body that's wet, goes down with a fantastic head - Holden's Black Country Bitter, beautiful. Oo er missus !* I'll have some of what he's on. Jimmy of Dudley says *the match day special is bostin!* It is a very good real ale pub.

56 Sandwell Rd B70 8TJ
G Pat and Julie Patel
F Full menu most of the week, reduced on matchdays but Indian snacks and rolls available
T 0121 5254600
S Two non smoking and two smoking areas, good ventilation and cleaners.

BWV 22.2.05 Archers **Golden Ale,** Pardoes **Entire,** Malvern Hills **Dr. Gillys Winter Ale,** Wessex **Kilmington,** Thatchers **Cider.**

This pub is a throwback to how I *imagined* they were in the 70's. retaining traditional values in the seating, décor and quality of service. in this truly friendly side street local. The pub is not only for Baggies friendships, *we have Blues, Villa, Wolves and Walsall and the rapport is fantastic (Geoff Clarke of Wednesbury)* Pat and the customers *welcome good beer, good food and good humour from all who call in, whatever their team. (David Davies),* You can see the obvious family ties with the food ethos found at the Vine, *(As Ron of West Bromwich says it has a good friendly atmosphere for home and away supporters to toast a good result with award winning ales* The Midland pub co and Evening Star plaudits are well deserved as they say, this is *the perfect pub.*

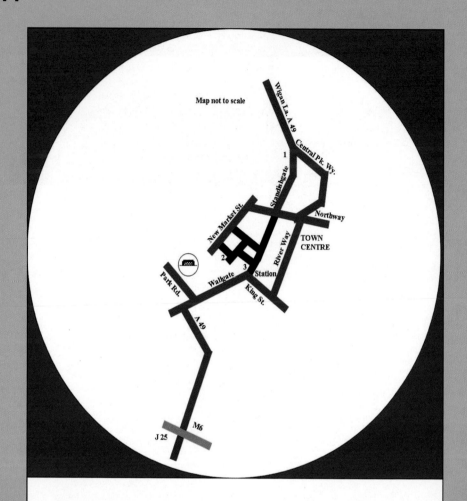

Wigan

The geniality of the Wigan pub drinker extends to them *having no loyalty card for their locals*. Who would blame the real ale drinker who has plenty of choice of pubs liberally scattered across the town and within the individual communities. I try here to give you a flavour of what is on offer.

Wigan

1 Bowling Green Trust Inns	2 Anvil Freehouse	3 Swan and Railway W + D

sp	tv	bm	pg	mp	sk	bm	d	mp	tv	bm	pg	d

108 Wigan Lane, WN1 2LF
G Mark Saunders
F From 12
T 01942 516004
S Smoking throughout

BWV 1.3.05 Caledonian **80/-,
Deuchars IPA,** Greene King **Old Speckled Hen,** Tetley's **Cask Bitter, Dark Mild.**

This rejuvenated pub has recently won a CAMRA award, and it is obvious to see why. It is a positively *anti smooth* hostelry offering a range of quality nationals supplemented by regional guests. Essentially a home of League fans the pub is typical of Wigan in having a mobile fan base. The *socially cosmopolitan regulars* enjoy a place where the care of the beer and what goes on in the pub sets the tone. Log fires for those who seek a bit of comforting, breakfast menus for those more active clients thinking of seeking other pursuits. The Pub has many features of note that include the curious screened route to the toilets, and beautiful separate vaults and lounge. It is indeed worthy of a film set ala "Early Doors" or perhaps a sequel to the Titanic, as this is an *ocean liner lounge* of a pub. *The food is good enough for the local Sandwich maker to come in for his repast.* All in all a pub that will do the premiership proud.

Dorning St. WN1 1ND
G Ian Thorpe
F Pub menu before game, restaurant after
T 01942 239444
S Smoking throughout

BWV 1.3.05 Hydes **Anvil, Dark Mild.** Roosters **Yankee,** Phoenix **Arizona,** Merlin **Cannonball,**

A great ;pub should leave you wanting to return and the Anvil did this in spade loads. There are always 2 or 3 guests hunted down by Ian for his lucky regulars. They certainly appreciate it, *a beltin' beer, beltin' staff, beltin atmosphere. Bloody beltin' pub* (John of Wigan) The pub is brightly decorated in light pine yet has other areas off the bar that retain the carpet and comfy chair feeling. Another feature is the range of 7 Belgian beers on tap. The award winning landlord is indeed proactive as the myriad of CAMRA certificates on bar proclaim. This genuine Freehouse is by all measures a great pub with a great landlord. *Nice beer, nice atmosphere (Stan of Wigan)* that *never disappoints (Nick)* Get there and enjoy the values that make this pub so good. As Norman says *Top marks!* for this pub *with a well controlled, convivial atmosphere (Nick of Burnley)* with *cask ale that is more consistent than my football team (Kaye of Wigan).*

80 Wallgate WN 1 1BA
G Alan Pardoe
F From 12
T 01942 495032
S Separate smoking sections

BWV 1.3.05 Banks' **Bitter, Original,** Titanic **Captain Smith's,** Everards **Original.**

To complete the Wigan beer fest a visit to the Swan and Railway is a must. It is a real footie lovers pub that offers architectural glory as well as good ale. The Latics fans describe this as *home.* No wonder, as Alan goes the extra mile top make both home and away fans welcome. From a designated Latics back room to breakfast related meetings of the faithful, the pub has become the focal point for those traveling away as well as meeting before the match. This listed building has seen hard times, including a recent fire but retains its splendour. While there try to answer these S+R trivia questions What is the mistake in the ornate stained glass window above the bar? What is the signature mark of the original Victorian tiler? Who are the Railway Children and have you met them in this pub? Book early if you want to stay here, the accommodation is being refurbished as I write, what could be more convenient, the main line is literally at your window.

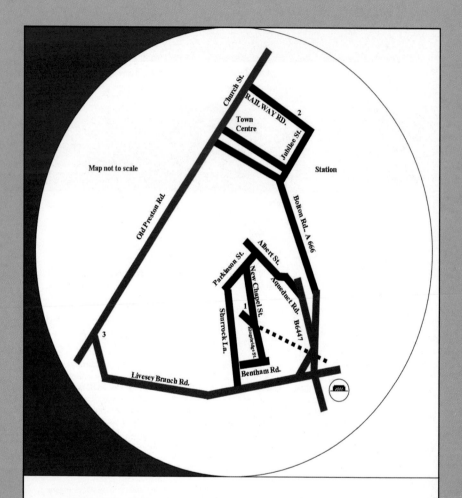

Blackburn

As Thwaites' adverts say "Not everything up north is grim."
With careful searching you can find enthusiasm for real ale especially when 3 B's Brewery ales are on offer. Most pubs lie around King St. in the town centre, my selection offers variety including a canal walk to Ewood.

1 Navigation Thwaites   2 The Adelphi Enterprise   3 Fieldens Arms

| sp | tv | bm | pg | | mp | tv | bm | pg | | sp | tv | bm | pg |

2 Canal St, BB2 4DL
G Barbara Hickey
T 01254 53230
S Smoking throughout.

BWV 22.11.04 Thwaites **Bitter, Mild**

A friendly canal side local with a short walk to the ground, this pub is often found by away fans. The two original bars retain their Victorian local character and offer quality ale rather than a wide range. I loved sampling Thwaites ales in a Thwaites pub, particularly the mild at Northern prices. The pub also offers a pool table and welcoming locals. Home of the London branch of the Blackburn Rovers Supporters club. who meet in the right hand bar. it is well known for being the pub for a good mix of home and away fans, just as it should be. It didn't take long to strike up a conversation with the friendly bar flies. Their recommendation was a stroll along the canal to the game and of course to return afterwards to continue a post match post mortem. Anyone coming by Canal? Thought not, but perhaps a summer holiday stopping off point maybe? The Navigation would be my pub of choice in Blackburn because it offers a touch of quality away from the masses who roam the town only to find the usual large keg houses or theme pubs.

22 Railway Rd, BB1 1EZ
G Lynn Balshaw
F From 11
T 01254 681128
S Smoking throughout

BWV 22.11.04 3 B's **Bobbins Bitter**, Black Sheep **Bitter**, Jennings **Cocker Hoop.**

This town centre local pub has high ceilings, ornate fireplaces and comfortable carpeted seating areas off the main bar. It has a genuine Victorian feel and is popular with those enjoying a quick pint and meal before catching a bus or train as well as local regulars. I particularly enjoyed the fact that at lunchtime there was a good splattering of single elderly females in small groups who found this pub relaxing enough to stop off for a meal in while in town. The choice of ale included the local Three B's Bobbins Bitter and while in Blackburn it would be rude not to sample plenty, the choice changes but their beers are usually available. Some town centre pubs work as a real local without the need for gimmicks such as happy hours, themes etc. The Adelphi is one such pub. The footie fan will find a place near to the station that is large enough to take the bigger groups yet with plenty of places to sit quietly discussing the game without being particularly obvious.

673 Old Preston Rd BB2 5ER
G Steve Johnson
F From 12
T 01254 200988
S Smoking throughout

BWV 22.11.04 Archers **Goodwill,** Boddingtons **Cask,** 3 B's **Stokers Slake** , Flowers **IPA,** Tetley's **Dark Mild**

It would be very difficult to miss this large Victorian village local as you arrive along the Old Preston Road. It is beautiful pub, and the pride of Steve and his wife. In fact my opening time visit was just a few days after local regular Steve had bought the pub, he liked it so good. Vying for his attention was the brewer from 3 B's Brewery just around the corner. First pub and a potential session looming, the chat was both fun, informative and set me upon a great day in the Blackburn area. Friendliness or what? With an emphasis on sparkling quality the pub will doubtless go through changes that build on its deservedly good reputation. There were plenty of choices of where to set up a group beer tasting. I would prefer the wood paneled room complete with cottage pub paraphernalia. The locals are very much local, augmented by those on the way to or from the brewery making it a place that has genuine interest for real ale fans,

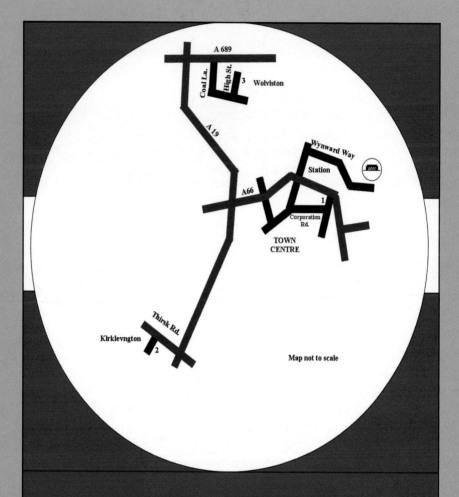

Map not to scale

Middlesbrough

The image of Middlesbrough is such that many fans go straight to the stadium and get away as soon as they can afterwards. Real ale fans should do the same as the choice is very limited. My advice is to find a good country pub.

1 Doctor Browns Enterprise   2 Crown Hotel Avebury Taverns   3 Ship

mp   sk   bm   pg   cp   bm   pg   sp   pg

135 Corporation Rd, TS1 3BZ
F From 12 (Not matchdays)
T 01642 213213
S Smoking throughout

BWV 13.1.05 Caledonian **Deuchars IPA**, Black Sheep **Bitter,** Greene King **Old Speckled Hen**

When I visited everything was changing; the beers, the landlord, the weather, everything. It looks great, a triangular street corner bar with interesting bar architecture. It is very light and welcoming and buzzes on matchdays. I hope the changes don't include losing real ale. It is easy to say it is the best, it is probably the only real ale pub in town, however it is and the ale is good. Convenient for the station and the riverside walk to the ground, it gets very busy on matchdays when the town springs into life. My visit also found several groups of young ale drinkers sharing tales of student life and the merits of local microbrews. All very heartening as was the ease of conversation over the lack of alternatives within the city ale scene. The CAMRAguide talks of Boro piping their own T.V. coverage of the games to the pub and the reputation the Doctors has for live music at the weekend. For me it was a seat in the window watching the locals trudging by, probably looking for a lager!

Thirsk Rd. Kirklevington TS15 9LT
G Alison Kirkwood and Barry Jackson
F From 12
T 01642 780044
S Smoking in bar.

BWV 13.1.05 John Smiths **Magnet**

This is a tasteful refurbishment of a pub with a growing reputation. It is a magnet on matchdays for far flung Boro' fans returning home. A small cellar means Barry concentrates on quality rather than quantity and very good it is too. There is a second ale on at weekends. Alison has created a great community pub, putting the locals into the centre of village life even though the location is out of the centre on the "main road" The pub will continue to improve because it welcomes those who value good food and real ale. Not a pub for the big coach load, definitely one for the family. The country pub feel is not overdone, nor the move towards good freshly cooked food. In the middle of winter the attraction of an open fire to warm myself before heading off to the joys of Teesside winds sounds pretty good. So too is the instant friendship of the Boro fans who have also endured the delights of the A1 / A19 wagon train experience.

50 The High St. Wolviston, TS22 5JX
G Edna Sanderson
F From 12
T 01740 644420
S Smoking throughout

BWV 13.1.05 Greene King **Old Speckled Hen**, Black Sheep **Bitter**

This pub is also convenient for travelers to Hartlepool being in the centre of a small village just south of the A689 / A19 junction. Wolviston is a pretty "green village" with another pub opposite to offer some variety should you want to do the full Wolviston bit. This traditional village hostelry offers a choice of national ales that are ever rotating, usually within two days. With no music and a wide range of food, it is very relaxing. The food and ale menu reflects Edna's enjoyment of her craft. Freshly cooked and "worth the wait" food is the speciality. My recommendation of the Ship is partly because I am imagining people making a weekend of the visit by staying in Durham or Newcastle and then might venture south on the morning of the game. We would have done the same, finding a good country pub, just the two of us, before going on to meet the lads at the game or in town. This is not a pub for coach loads or large groups of lads.

Championship Category winners

	Pub	Town
Within 10 minutes to the ground	Bridge Bier Haus	Burnley
Pub for food	Fellows, Morton and Clayton	Nottingham
Brewery Tap	Vat and Fiddle	Nottingham
Street corner local	Dove	Ipswich
Town High Street / Station boozer	Hobgoblin	Reading
Historic pub	Whitelocks	Leeds
Microbrew champion	Kelham Island Tavern	Sheffield
Footie fans pub	Lord Nelson	Brighton
Pub with a view	The Dove	London
Community pub	Kings Arms	Sunderland
Loads of real ale pub	Brunswick	Derby

Championship
Pub of the year 2004 - 05

The award goes to the pub which meets most of the criteria above.

FELLOWS, MORTON AND CLAYTON

Nottingham

Sheffield

1 Kelham Island Tavern	2 Ship Inn Hardy and Hansons	3 Fat Cat Freehouse

sp   pg   sp   tv   bm   pg   sp

1 Kelham Island Tavern

62 Russell St. S3 8RW
G Trevor Wraith
F Traditional bar snacks and full menu available from 12 to 3.
T 0114 2722482
S Separate smoking and non smoking areas
W www.kelhamislandtavern.co.uk

BWV 14.3.05 Pictish **Brewers Gold,** Acorn **Barnsley Bitter,** Ossett **Silver King,** Arkells **3B,** Archers **Predator,** Glentworth **Yorkshire Light Ale,** Leydon **On me head son!** Rudgate **Happy Masher,** Westons **Old Rosie Cider,** Saxon **Ruby Tuesday, Platinum Blonde.**

The local pub of the year is the obvious starting point for the Kelham Island crawl. There is a danger you might not leave though. It is a spotless haunt of the chattering classes and my visit soon found the locals in full flow, topics ranging from politics to mediaeval history. The pub extends backwards into the courtyard where the reason for the Yorkshire in Bloom awards become evident in the small garden. The pub has a classy style, festooned with classic art work and classic ale choices. *A top boozer that all will enjoy, a beautiful bar with beautiful beer.* The pub is rightly a regular beer award winner, one cannot be less impressed by not only the range of ales, but their quality.

2 Ship Inn

312 Shalesmoor S1 2DS
G Steve Hodgson
T 0114 2812204
S Smoking throughout

BWV 14.3.05 Hardy and Hansons **Bitter.**

To meet all needs of the genuine real ale crawler any local area needs some pubs of supplement the microbrew style ale houses, The Ship offers quality ale in an pub not geared to up mass real ale ticking. It is a locals pub, having pool tables, T.V. and attention given to the regulars needs. It is simply furnished in a style that we all recognise from a 80's new wave style refurbishment. The layout is of a single room around a smaller than usual bar. What you have then is a good boozer that will suit the bitter drinker who seeks Hardy and Hanson ale when venturing North. I liked the pub, perhaps because it did normal pub things i.e. my visit found a pool match in full swing. Very quickly you get to find the routine of a community local pub. The Guv'nor and his wife make you welcome as soon as you come through the door, and pints are pulled as if by magic within seconds of what might be the regulars same time of arrival every night. This pub is a must on the Kelham Island ale trail, especially as the first or last before the tram journey.

3 Fat Cat

23 Alma Road S3 8SA
G David Wickett
F From 12
T 0114 2494801
S Separate smoking areas
W www.the fat cat.co.uk

BWV 14.3.05 Kelham Island **Pale Rider, Best, Easy Rider,** Fat Cat **Bitter,** Salamander **Blunderbus,** Hart Cartford **Premium,** Durham **Nine Stars,** Cottage **Evening Star,** Acorn **Legend.**

This is the most quaint and original of the three Fat Cats in these guides As the Kelham Island tap room alone it would gain a national fame without the name. It is a tiny pub with two small rooms, one being quite separate and smoke free. Both have a highly polished and well cared for quality, suggesting that the comfort of the punters is as important as the high quality and diverse ales. Add in a distinctive menu and you have a pub that appeals to couples in their middle ages as well as the older crew found in traditional ale houses. The leader of the Sheffield revolution it has managed to maintain the highest of standards as the numerous awards testify. I loved the humourous touches, for example gents cannot miss the "Great Urinals of Sheffield." This is a great pub that has a *must not miss element.*

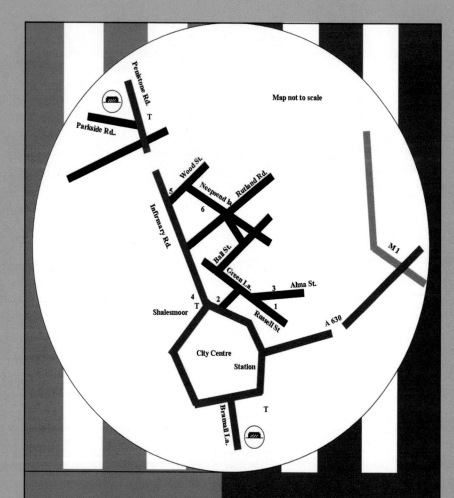

Map not to scale

Sheffield

The location of 6 really good ale houses are shown on the map and you may notice none are near the ground. This is because the Shalesmoor area is just so good it would be a real ale drinkers crime not to seek them out. Add in many town centre locations and some near Bramall Lane and Hillsborough and we have the near perfect footie and real ale town.

4 Cask and Cutler Freehouse ### 5 Hillsborough Hotel Freehouse ### 6 Gardeners Rest Freehouse

sp   d   sp   tv   pg   sp   pg   d

1 Henry St. S3 7EQ
G Neil Clarke
T 0114 2492295
S Separate non smoking room

BWV 14.3.05 E+S **Old Gimmer,** Whitley Bridge **Bridge Gold, Emberzale.** Pictish **Brewers Gold,** Millstone **Windy Miller,** Hart **Cartford,** Salamander **Stout,** Westons **Old Rosie Cider**

The most recommended of the local pubs the Cask and Cutler is located at the end of the local Shalemoor tram stop. Or conversely Gary S of Sheffield says *it offers a constantly changing range of excellently kept real ales within staggering distance of the tram stop taking you to the Mecca of football - Hillsborough.* Dynamic, yet traditional, small but large of heart, I would challenge anyone not to think this pub is perfectly formed. The two rooms are equally private, being screened by the internal walls and woodwork. The pubs offers unusual ales that constantly change plus Belgian bottled ales. Nicola S of Barnsley has it right, *It keeps my husband occupied with the plethora of real ales whilst I hit the shops!* There are no themes or music, just regulars chatting or planning an evening that, on my visit, involved bringing a bottle to carry home the ale.

54 - 58 Langsett Road
G Carlo Jamieson
F From 6
S Smoking to the rear of pub.
T 0114 2322100
W www.edalebrewery.co.uk

BWV 14.3.05 Edale **Kinder Stouter, Ringing Roger,** Crown **HPA, Loxley Gold, Stannington Stout,** Wellington **Old Nosey, Volenti,** Archers **County of Wiltshire.**

The Hillsborough is a working hotel offering good value, room only accommodation and organic food. The interest for us, however. will be the ales that are brewed below the pub under the three names found here. Of interest to serious ale lovers will be the attempts to recreate brews of old through the *revival* recipes. The pub does many different things really well. The placing of smoking areas in the conservatory overlooking the Don Valley is both simple, allowing all to enter a smoke free pub, and enlightening, I loved the large breakfast room style bar to the left and could happily go back and enjoy the river views when needed. (Views of the Mecca Bingo hall actually) You should not miss this pub, on the tram line, it is a classic of how to combine ale and hotel without the compromise of losing drinking or smoking space.

105 Neepend lane
G Pat Wilson and Eddie Munnelly
T 0114 224978
S Separate non smoking room

BWV 14.3.05 Timothy Taylor **Landlord, Best, Golden Best,** Wentworth **Needle's Eye,** Greenfield **Pride Of England, Castleshaw,** Houston's **Horny Wee Devil,** Bowland **Malmsey Butt,** Westons **Old Rosie, Herefordshire Country Perry.**

And so to my personal favourite in the Sheffield crawl. Instantly the locals made it obvious that this was a pub for those who value matters local in ale and life. They offer regular ales, ever changing guests, ale selection on gravity and ciders. I once was an Geographer so I went into the conservatory that has planning maps to find a view of the Don undergoing its rejuvenation. In the bar I claimed my place on the map over the bar. Soon it became a conversation with Tim, author of the guide to Sheffield pubs and the tour of the area could easily have ended here as the warmth of the place was just perfect. The front snug is quite separate from the rest of the pub. The ultimate accolade came when local brewers came in for a pint. The People of Sheffield don't know just how lucky they are.

Division One Category winners

	Pub	Town
Within 10 minutes to the ground	Palmerston arms	Peterborough
Pub for food	Arden Arms	Stockport
Brewery Tap	Whalebone	Hull
Street corner local	Victoria (Dunstable)	Luton
Town High Street / Station boozer	Ashton Inn	Oldham
Historic pub	Station Tavern	Huddersfield
Microbrew champion	Fighting Cock	Bradford
Footie fans pub	Jacksons Wharf	Hartlepool
Pub with a view	Crown	Wrexham
Community pub	Crown and Sceptre	Torquay
Loads of real ale pub	Derby Tup	Chesterfield

Pub of the year 2004 - 05

The award goes to the pub which meets most of the criteria above.

ARDEN ARMS

STOCKPORT

1 Ratepayers Arms Freehouse

2 Wellington Arms Bath Ales

3 Cornubia Smiles Pub. Co.

cp   tv   pg   d   cp   d   sp   pg

Filton Leisure Centre, BS34 7 PS
G John Beese
T 01454866697
F From 12

BWV 6.12.04 Otter **Claus**, Butcombe **Bitter**, Charles Wells **Bombardier**, Ind Coope **Burton Ale**, Stonehenge **Great Bustard**.

If you know that Bristol has masses of choice but plenty of associated transport hassles then the Ratepayers offers an interesting alternative. This is a suburban leisure centre bar owned by the local council. In a rare act of enlightened thinking John has been given license to create a real ale bar with a great range of good quality ales. In a typical café / bar style you find a lounge bar that is a really good locals dropping off point. Of course it is frequented by athletic and not so athletic types, the former having played squash, badminton etc, the latter, like me dreaming of past energies and revelling in the real ale. It offers simple food and is welcoming to all ages. The selection of ales specialises in regional microbrews yet has national well-known brands for the less adventurous. Unique as an entry in these guides, it might encourage a local person to take up physical activity, well perhaps not, cribbage or darts while enjoying good ale is enough for me.

Gloucester Rd, BS7 8UR
G Paul Tanner
T 0171 9513022
F Bacon, sausage sandwiches chips cheese + full evening menu
S No smoking at the bar and one non smoking room.

BWV 12.4.05 Bath **Gem, Spa, Barnstormer**, 3 Rivers **Disreputable**.

My final pub of the 270 or odd visited was purposely selected because I wanted to finish on a pub of real quality. Recently bought by Bath Ales, the "Welly" is well known in Footie and real ale circles for *the quality of its beers and the friendliness of its customers / staff*. The pub is a grand old saloon with palatial Victorian architecture. It is also labelled home only, so it is best to get there early without colours. You will be made welcome. *Its gert lush! (Ian).* The pub gets very busy on match days, perhaps best so when the "Bris" are "heaving" before a Rugger match. As Grant Buckley says *When you stumble out the door it's a two minute roll down the hill to the ground plus there is top totty behind the bar!*, Most will linger longer comforted by the fact that the range of ales and ciders will satisfy most needs and more. This acts as a *good anaesthetic before the dross on the pitch. (Gary K)*

142 Temple St. BS1 6EN
G Julia Richardson
T 0117 9254415
S Smoking throughout

BWV 12.4.05 Otter **Bitter**, Spinning Dog **Mutley Springer**, Palmers **Tally Ho!** Smiles **IPA**, Archers **Bouncing Bunnies**, Cottage **Western Glory**, Bristol Ciderworks **Cider**.

This pub is perfect for weekenders or those returning to the station after the game. The nationally famous Cornubia is not open on Saturday lunchtime. Set back from a side road off Victoria St you have to imagine pre Blitz Bristol to understand its location among the city office blocks and brewery townscape. The Cornubia is a fantastic boozer that has the qualities that I value highly in the best of British ale houses. A simple layout of bar and no frills, an open fire place to toast yourself in winter, a pub front with tables to spill out onto hot summers days. Pickled eggs on the bar, indicators of cerebral pastimes behind it and a fantastic choice of ales. Smiles may have gone as an independent brewer but the Cornubia lives on in spirit and quality. On the Real ale trail, it attracts tickers from the station and office workers at lunchtime. It is Weekend evenings that see it heaving, so get there early.

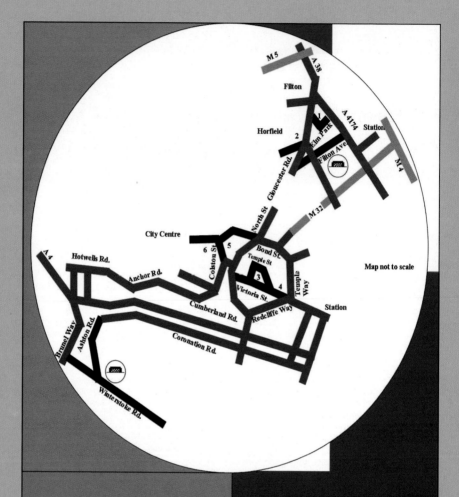

Bristol

There are several really good pubs with real ale in the Hor-field area. Many however, will make a weekend of the stay in Bristol so the Cornubia offers a starting point for an excellent city crawl. What you need is for Rovers to be promoted every year so that the joys of Bristol can be shared around.

Bristol Centre

4 Kings Head Enterprise   5 Brewery Tap Freehouse   6 Zerodegrees Freehouse

mp   mp   bm   sp   sky   bm   d

4 Kings Head

Victoria St BS1 6DE
G Jane Wakeham
S Smoking throughout
T 0117 9277860

BWV 12.4.05 Sharps **Cornish Coaster**, **Doom Bar.** Courage Best, Bass,

Leaving Temple Meads the first pub you will notice on Victoria St. looks like an antique shop on the outside and, some might say, on the inside as well. It is a great starting (or better, finishing) point to a tour of Bristol. The Kings Head is a low ceiling narrow single bar of National Historic importance. The Courage window is now historic in its own right since the Brewery and the associated aroma has long since gone. The pubs' reputation relies upon the quality and selection of ales, often featuring west country ales. The place quickly fills up with a great combination of office workers in the day, joined by real ale fans in the afternoon / evening and distant regulars in the evening. Nowhere is far from the bar so it would be difficult not to be noticed here. It is very small and totally friendly. If you are a fan of a bigger club, just check in advance because, due to its convenient location between the station and City Centre, it will sometimes be closed on match days.

5 Brewery Tap

6 - 10 Colston St. BS1 5BD
G Matt Mason
T 0117 9213668
F From 11.30

BWV 12.4.05 Smiles **Heritage, Best, Bristol IPA,** Wickwar Cotswold Way.

Smiles brewing may have joined Courage as being lost to Bristol but the Smiles Company Brewery Tap continues the traditions of this innovative and much loved Bristol beer trend setter. Other local ales will undoubtedly come to take prominence over the months but the comfort and originality of this pub continues to be popular with people of all ages and outlooks. My lunchtime visit found mostly women in the bar; nurses, office meetings, groups of people taking a drink between the town and tourist business. The layout means that you can usually find solitude in one of the back wooden walled rooms or join in more pubby chat at the bar at the front. I like the use of hop sacks on the wall and the general feeling of well planned disorganisation within the rustic furniture. This is a gentle lunchtime pub that gives way to young and old planning nights out in town in the evening. A great pub in a good location and with, one hopes, a bright if now less Smiles dependent future.

6 Zerodegrees

53 Colston Street BS1 5BA
G Stephen Holman
F Pizzas, mussels, pasta, salads and gourmet sausages (Sunday roast)
T 01179252706
S Non smoking in restaurant.
W www.zerodegrees.co.uk

BWV 12.4.05 Zerodegrees **Pilsner, Pale Ale, Black Lager, Wheat Ale, Special.**

Have you been to an American style, microbrew, or perhaps, a new German Tavern? Maybe you might have found an architect designed London warehouse serving good ale. The new Zerodegrees has arrived in Bristol and has made an immediate impression on the real ale scene. The sparkling nature of the brewery and its industrial interior make an instant impact. The beer is the ultimate of instant access, direct from the stills to the glass. Add in plasma screens for both big Rugby and Footie matches and you get a wider appeal than merely a trendy bar. The pub has a minimalist look yet still makes me feel like I am welcome as an occasional visitor. After a chat with Martin, the head brewer of German descent, I retired to the balcony in perfect contentment and set off going through the list. Be sure to ask what the special is, it will often surprise, much as the Black lager excites.

Division Two Category winners

	Pub	Town
Within 10 minutes to the ground	Wellington	Bristol
Pub for food	Three Horseshoes	High Wycombe
Brewery Tap	Zerodegrees	Bristol
Street corner local	Kemble Tavern	Cheltenham
Town High Street / Station boozer	Waters Green Tavern	Macclesfield
Historic pub	Cemetery Hotel	Rochdale
Microbrew champion	Number Twenty 2	Darlington
Footie fans pub	Rose and Crown	Bury
Pub with a view	Railway (Killay)	Swansea
Community pub	Railway (Wheatley)	Oxford
Loads of real ale pub	Three Fishes	Shrewsbury

Pub of the year 2004 - 05

The award goes to the pub which meets most of the criteria above.

CEMETERY HOTEL

ROCHDALE

1 Three Fishes Enterprise 2 Coach and Horses Freehouse 3 Admiral Benbow Freehouse

mp   mp   bm   mp

Fish St Sy1 1UR
G David Moss
F From 12
T 01743 344793
S No smoking throughout

BWV 19.11.04 Caledonian **Deuchars IPA,** Timothy Taylor **Landlord,** Downton **Raspberry Wheat,** Fullers **London Pride**

This award winning pub is in an historic street near to Gay Meadow the landlord has created a pub for a wide range of drinkers. This Three Fishes is an instant recommendation whenever I talk to fans about pubs in this town. A small, one bar pub, beautifully kept real ales and with a no smoking policy that is the pub USP. The beams and hanging hops add to the bucolic feel. The choice of guest ales offer some great surprises and are evidently popular with the regulars. During the day it is quite a tourist and office workers haunt, in the evening the locals take over. The regulars were very keen to give me advice on what makes a good pub and a good pint. *If a beer isn't quite to your liking don't panic another one will be on soon, talk to David and you might even get to choose.* Every time I go there I find something better to tell my friends about, usually related to the dry humour that pervades in every conversation in the pub.

Swan Hill SY1 1NF
G Ross Ireland
F From 12
T 01743 365661
S Separates smoking areas

BWV 19.11.04 Salopian **Shropshire Gold, Shropshire Icon,** Cheddar **Vale Cider,** Boddingtons **Bitter,** Three Tuns **Toddly Tom**

Two bars and three separate rooms make up this atmospheric ale house. The Coach and Horses champion local brews and have a tradition of welcoming away real ale fans. The pub rotates its guest beers and imported lagers and has the room for groups of varying sizes. The selection leans towards local microbrews but also includes continental lagers and always a real cider. *There are plenty of places to hide away if you fancy a quieter time.* This will be the case on a normal non match day perhaps. The pub will have its fair share of CAMRA members and town beer hunters mixed in with tourists wanting a pub out of the main high street business. On match days get there early to do it justice. The Salopian ales made a great find for me as they are rarely found on my travels. The chat with the bar man and locals set me up for the rest of the day. The Coach and Horses is a top pub in a top town.

Swan Hill SY1 1NF
G Mike Vaughan
T 01743 2444423
S Separate smoking areas

BWV 19.11.04 Six Bells **Big Nev's, Cloud Nine,** John Roberts **Three Tuns,** Hanby **Bull Rush,** Salopian **Choir Porter,** Greene King **IPA**

Leaving the Coach and Horses and heading downhill you then come across the Admiral Benbow, a complementary pub that has to be sampled. This is a two bar "traditional" pub specialising in local brews, finding the smaller brewers and giving them a great outlet in town., It has an over 25's policy that sets it apart and helps to create an atmosphere all of its own, described as *relaxed yet bubbly.* If on a crawl I would start and finish here because the range and quality stands out. On my visit the afternoon office party crowd were ending an all afternoon session. It is a good location for this as they were able to find a back area of the pub totally to their self leaving the regulars and serious ale heads to do the usual supping and chatting in the cosy front bar. It was a great place for both groups to treat the pub as their own. Three great pubs and not a visit to Loggerheads as yet, Shrewsbury just has too much choice.

It takes all sorts to campaign for real ale

Join CAMRA Today...

Just fill in the form below and send, with a cheque (payable to CAMRA ltd) or for Three Months Free membership (for those renewing or joining by Direct Debit) complete the Direct Debit Form. All forms should be addressed to membership secretary, CAMRA, 230 Hatfield Road, St Albans, Herts, AL1 4LW. Alternatively you can join online at www.camra.org.uk. Rates for single membership are £18 and joint £21. Concession rates are available on request.

....
Title   Surname   Forename(s)   Date of Birth
....
P'tner Surname   Forename(s)   Date of Birth
....
Address   Postcode

Tel. no.(s)

I wish to join the Campaign for Real Ale, and agree to abide by the Memorandum and Articles of Association.

I enclose a cheque for........... Signed.. Date ....

Applications will be processed within 21 days

Season 2004 - 05 League tables.
Ranking of towns based on number of real ale pubs and their friendliness to away fans

PREMIERSHIP	CHAMPIONSHIP	DIVISION 1	DIVISION 2
Newcastle		Stockport	Shrewsbury
	Sheffield	Peterborough	Nottingham
Norwich	Derby	Sheffield	Bristol
	London	Bristol	Lincoln
London	Nottingham	Swindon	London
	Sunderland	Huddersfield	Darlington
Manchester	Ipswich	Bradford	Macclesfield
	Brighton	Oldham	Cambridge
Liverpool	Reading	Hull	Chester
	Plymouth	Chesterfield	Boston
Bolton	Cardiff	Torquay	Oxford
	Gillingham	Brentford	Kidderminster
Portsmouth	Preston	Port Vale	Cheltenham
	Wolverhampton	Hartlepool	Grimsby
Birmingham	Leicester	Luton	Bury
	Leeds	Milton Keynes	Rochdale
Southampton	Wigan	Bournemouth	Swansea
	Watford	Walsall	Northampton
West Bromwich	Burnley	Doncaster	Southend
	Coventry	Blackpool	Rushden
Blackburn	Crewe	Wrexham	Mansfield
	Stoke	Tranmere	Scunthorpe
Middlesbrough	Rotherham	Barnsley	Yeovil
		Colchester	Wycombe

Fancy writing for a Stedders Guide?
Or
Writing descriptions of real ale pubs?
Maybe
Getting paid for visiting pubs and talking real ale?
Does this
Sound too good to be true?

There are several ways that you can be involved in Stedders Guides.

Yes you can;-

- Complete a card in a pub to comment on a pub, 400 people did so for this years guides.
- Contribute by commenting on www.footballandrealaleguide.co.uk
- Email me at Richard@footballandrealaleguide.co.uk

But

The real fun is to be paid to join the team.

So

I am looking to create a small team of part time contributors for the football and real ale guide 2006 -07 and in the future similar guides for Rugby / Cricket and Real ale guides in the Stedders Guide format.

You must be:-

- a real ale fan
- have knowledge of the needs of away fans when they visit a new town.
- able and willing to travel independently to parts of the country at times other than when following football to chat to landlords and local people.
- have good I.T. skills and be contactable via email and telephone.
- able to work to strict deadlines.
- willing to share the fun of footie and real ale in your writing and conversation.

If this is you and you can organise your other commitments to get involved then why not apply for a job working with me on next years guides.

Any post will be on a part time basis and will include either expenses or a bursary related to the number of entries and sales of future guides.

The posts would suit someone who has the time to work outside of their full time occupation.

OR

Perhaps you are seeking a change in life direction that involves having time to manage your own work /leisure time.

IN OCTOBER 2005 I WILL BE ADVERTISING FOR TEAM MEMBERS

Application forms will be available from September 2005.

GET IN EARLY,

CONTACT ME TO DISCUSS THE JOBS AND POSSIBLE RENUMERATION at

r.stedman1@btinternet.com

Or

01844 343931

Frog Island Brewery

Northampton

| Fire-bellied Toad 5% | Best Bitter 3.5 % | Natterjack 4.8% | Shoemaker 4.2% |

When in the East Midlands the Brewery ales to search for is;-

Frog Island Brewery

**The Maltings
Westbridge
St. James Road
Northampton
NN5 5HS**

**www.frogislandbrewery.co.uk
Contact
Tel. 01604 750754
Fax 01299 270260**